CAPTURED
VOICES

CAPTURED VOICES

An anthology of poems and prose

Presented by John McCarthy

Edited by Janna Letts and Fiona Whytehead

Victor Gollancz
LONDON

First published in Great Britain in 1999 by
Victor Gollancz
An imprint of Orion Books Ltd
Orion House, 5 Upper St Martin's Lane, London WC2H 9EA

A CIP catalogue record for this book is available
from the British Library

ISBN 0575 06756 X

Typeset by Selwood Systems, Midsomer Norton
Printed and bound by
Butler & Tanner Ltd, Frome and London

Contents

PART III: IMPACT

PART IV: BYSTANDERS

PART V: SURVIVAL

PART VI: EXILE

Acknowledgements

The Medical Foundation for the Care of Victims of Torture, the editors and the publishers express their gratitude to the writers and other copyright holders who generously agreed to give us permission for the inclusion of their work for no fees.

In a few cases a small donation was given or a small fee was paid.

In some cases, names have been changed to protect people's identities.

All royalties from this book will go to the Medical Foundation for the Care of Victims of Torture to support its work.

Every effort has been made to trace the copyright holders of all the poems and extracts in this anthology. Any omission is unintentional and the editors and publishers would be pleased, if notified, to make any due acknowledgement in any future edition.

We would like to thank John McCarthy, patron of the Medical Foundation for his important contribution and for his support for this book right from the beginning. Also Mark Lucas, literary agent, for the initial idea to produce a book and his help in developing the project. We would also like to thank the staff and volunteers at the Foundation who have contributed in different ways: Sonja Linden, Writer-in-Residence, who carried out additional research, and Andrew Hogg, Press Officer, to whom the testimonies were told. Their work was invaluable in completing the book.

Also, from the Foundation, Richard McKane, Harriet Young, Rebecca Simor, Rachael Ward, Brita Melendez, Mena Gainpaulsingh and John Baguley.

Finally, we would like to give our thanks and appreciation to our editors at Gollancz: Humphrey Price for all his good advice and constant encouragement and Christine Kidney for guiding us through the final stages.

Janna Letts, Fiona Whytehead
The Medical Foundation for the Care of Victims of Torture 1999

Introduction

I was introduced to the Medical Foundation by Brian Keenan just over a year after I came back home from Lebanon. At a reception at the organization's headquarters in London, I found myself talking to a man who asked me how I was getting on back in the free world. I told him I felt fine, expecting him to go on, as so many other people had done, to say 'I can't begin to imagine what it was like in those awful prisons.' But he did not, he just smiled at me, a deep warmth in his eyes. I learned that he was from Argentina, that he had been a political prisoner for three years and that he had been tortured. I felt humbled. I had become too used to thinking of my experience as being virtually unique; too used to assuming that no one, apart from my fellow hostages, could really understand what it had been like. Yet here was a man who could immediately understand, and on a level far more profound than I could, to what depths the mind and body can be taken. As we talked, the feelings of humility diminished and I felt a great sense of calm and release sweeping through me.

Being home was all that I had dreamed of for over five years, but freedom had not proved initially as simply joyful as I had assumed it would. I was still nervous about going out, always preoccupied with minor concerns – would there be a throng of people, would I feel trapped, would there be a lavatory nearby? Often the simplest way to 'cope' was with too much alcohol.

I have received enormous support from all quarters to allow me a comfortable return into the real world. There were doctors for my body and my mind, there were business advisers and above all there were my family and friends, endlessly patient and gentle as I struggled to come to terms with the abrupt transfer from the bleak, dark world of captivity to the bright warmth of home and celebrity. Everyone I met was full of sensitive sympathy and those I most needed were always there for me.

Yet coming to terms with this was odd. Although I had grown up in a loving family environment and had had many good friendships, I was bowled over by the degree of warmth and unconditional consideration I received. I felt humbled and yet bemused, often irrationally suspicious of people's motives. It was strange to be treated with such respect. After a while I developed a love-hate relationship with this; enjoying and expecting attention and understanding, while often resenting it and wanting only to be left alone.

When people did say 'I can't imagine what it was like', I would reply with one of a few stock responses: 'Oh, well, once you get used to it you can cope . . . I was lucky to have been held with such good men . . . Actually, once you've adjusted, the main problem is boredom . . . ' and so on. The conversation could then take off again, avoiding the real suffering, the terrors and depressions, despair and humiliations, and I would talk of the games we played, the plans we made, focusing on the value of our friendships, emphasizing the strengths found and developed rather than what we had lost.

To some degree I think this was a result of the confusion I felt about my experience, almost as if I too could not imagine what we had suffered: as if it was just that, imagined and not a reality.

I was also wary of appearing self-centred, maudlin, whingeing. After all, I had survived in good health and come home to a hero's welcome and great affection. What had I got to worry about?

Writing about the experience brought home what I had suffered. I was overcome with fear, raging anger and humiliation as I recalled incidents of abuse and casual cruelty and the long, blank, hopeless periods of nothing in a murky cell. Often I would recoil from the work, eager to block out the pain of remembered hurt. I was frightened of losing control, of being overwhelmed by the sorrow and confusion of those lost years and of being unable to cope with the rediscovered real world.

It took more than three years before I could let images and sensations flow through me without my swiftly switching to another mental channel. The process is still often difficult but now I can face the demons and gradually assimilate the wild mix of emotions that they promote.

This process, though, had been given good foundations from the moment I was freed. As soon as the blindfold came off, I was treated with great respect and gentle courtesy. I held a press conference: the world wanted to hear of my ordeal, was eager for all my news of the other hostages. The nightmare we had shared as a tiny part of Lebanon's misery was coming to an end at last.

The British ambassador in Damascus knew my family and friends and was able to give me some of their news as I waited for my father and brother to arrive on a special RAF flight to take us home to England. Once home I was provided with a secure, private and comfortable base and the chance to talk through what had happened. A team of psychologists were there to help me.

At first I had little to say about my life as a hostage; I felt I had come to terms with it all inside and, once out, I focused on getting back to the life I had known and picking up where I had left off five years earlier. I was given advice on how to cope with celebrity, with sudden memories of captivity and any difficult times that might develop with family and friends.

Despite such help, fogs of confusion still used to descend and cloud my thoughts. There was guilt about the men I had left behind in Lebanon; flashbacks to moments of shame and humiliation; confusion at the amount of interest in me and those nearest me.

But the main thing was that I was being asked and encouraged to talk through my experience. Often it seemed like pressure, but there was no attempt to control, rather they were trying to help me in expressing myself.

The clients of the Medical Foundation do not have this huge wave of general support and encouragement. For them there is no special plane to get them quickly to safety; to them uniforms cannot mean the security and pride of nationality that I knew – officials are more likely to be looking for reasons to send these victims back to the place of their torment. Often they have to struggle with a strange language, and live in fear in an alien culture, withstanding racist abuse as they mourn the loss of homeland and family. Most of these survivors have been physically and mentally tortured; not just beaten up, as I had been, but deeply and deliberately abused. They have seen their homes destroyed, witnessed their families hurt and often killed. Their abusers, their captors, had been their countrymen. Escape from oppression for them means loss of home. They must, if they are lucky, live in exile and try to come to terms with past horrors and present anxieties. The Medical Foundation is essential to their survival.

It is a remarkable place: a place where horror is confronted and contained. Contained, not in the sense of being bottled up, but of being safely identified and gradually put in a bearable context. Unspeakable atrocity can be revealed, acknowledged and allowed its own space. The survivors of torture find there a haven where they can talk through their experiences with interpreters and therapists with a wide range of skills. Many of the interpreters and caseworkers are themselves living in exile. They can share in their clients' memories: the fear of being moved, the abject shame at being unable to help other captives as they were beaten, the determination to maintain their dignity and the secret thoughts of vicious revenge against the captors. Together they can go back safely into those cells and remember with diminished horror the sanctuary they found when they were locked in alone. Yet there is no insistence that the clients talk, rather they are led along gently, encouraged to find their own time and way of speaking. The Medical Foundation is not a place of dogmas, of set therapies and formulas; indeed there is much debate over and experimentation with various techniques. There is no gradation of suffering – each case is given the attention it needs.

One evening I had a long conversation with Helen Bamber, the Foundation's director, about her organization's history. Our talk was regularly interrupted by raised voices followed by gales of laughter from the next room. Helen explained that this was a gathering of the allotments project, which involved more than twenty clients and their families working together to grow food and to regain a sense of independence and community. I remember Helen beaming as she recognized one woman's voice arguing with a man. The woman had been having enormous difficulties coming to terms with the loss of some of her family in her homeland while struggling to carry on in exile here. Clearly this allotments scheme, combined with more sophisticated counselling, was helping the woman live again.

The Medical Foundation developed out of the work Helen and others had been doing within Amnesty International. They documented the stories and injuries of torture victims for use in Amnesty's campaign to heighten public awareness of the problem worldwide – currently one hundred and seventeen countries use torture – and to lobby governments to use their influence with others to stop the practice.

This team came to realize that, though they could report on the horrors of torture and help with some of their clients' most urgent needs, they could not address the long-term problems the victims and their families faced in coming to terms with past experiences and a new life in this country. As a consequence the Medical Foundation was formed over the Christmas and New Year of 1985–86.

In its first year the Foundation saw seventy-nine people. To date its clinicians have seen 15,000 people, of whom 2,800 were new clients last year. The clients are referred from many sources – Amnesty International, the UN High Commission for Refugees, from hospitals, psychiatrists and lawyers.

There is now a paid staff of eighty, supported by over one hundred volunteers. Many of the volunteers are both highly skilled and qualified and include doctors, psychiatrists, caseworkers, psychotherapists, physiotherapists and social workers. Helen described the Foundation as 'a community to whom people feel they can turn with their terrible difficulties and feelings of being unable to go on'.

Most of the £3 million needed annually to keep the Medical Foundation running comes from individual donations and charitable trusts. Contributions are made by the UN and the European Union, to whom, in return, the Foundation makes reports on incidents of torture.

While the Medical Foundation is unique in this country in attending comprehensively to the needs of torture victims, it has been described as 'part of a mosaic, part of a whole group of organizations and individuals throughout the world who are involved in this struggle'. There is now an international lobby against torture but it is foolish to think that awareness and concern will see its end soon.

My voice was heard when I returned from Lebanon. This book is an opportunity for other voices to speak and be listened to. It is a collection of writing from people who have been imprisoned, tortured and lived in countries where atrocities were happening every day. In six sections – Loss, Identity, Impact, Bystanders, Survival and Exile – they achieve the difficult task of communicating the complexities of the thoughts and feelings of such experiences. Some of the writers are established, others unknown. Some are clients of the Foundation. One, Babek, came to the Foundation in 1986. His story takes us through the book.

I once asked Helen Bamber if she was proud of the Medical Foundation. 'When I see my colleagues struggling to find the truth, in themselves and in their work, I'm proud. I'm proud of the clinical developments we've made and the ways we've found to help our clients. The answers to the problems of torture lie elsewhere and we know that, but we can have an influence and that I'm proud of. But as an institution it shouldn't really be here and I don't want to lose sight of that. It ought not to exist today, really not.'

But it does, providing its clients with a vital platform to release their captured voices.

John McCarthy

Babek was one of the first clients of the Medical Foundation. He was a teacher who objected to his pupils, some as young as eight, being conscripted into the army and sent to war. His thoughts and feelings about his experiences begin each section of the book.

LOSS

People, beliefs and ideals can all be lost.

Babek

I used to write happy poems but I don't any more, I can't see happy colours, it is all just misery. They took away my fiancée; I was arrested on the night we had decided to get married and she was forced to marry someone else. My piece of land was confiscated and I was no longer allowed to teach. Former friends were afraid to speak to me and I could not live with my family because they would be in danger. My younger brother was killed in prison, he was only fifteen.

It is hard to feel happy because my people are not. I try because there are good things in my life now and I want to prove that I am alive and not a dead person. But when they stamped my hand on release from prison to say that I had my freedom I felt that they had taken my life away and that's what you get.

Perhaps the greatest loss is that trust is destroyed. That really hurts me. The government planted the seeds of hatred and the fruit of hatred is hatred.

Manuel José Arce

Manuel José Arce (1935–1985) was born in Guatemala and became one of its best-known and most influential playwrights and poets. Although he came from a local aristocratic family, he became an ardent supporter of the reformist Arbenz government, which was eventually overthrown by a CIA-based coup in 1954. Arce worked as a journalist and writer under extremely difficult conditions until he was forced to leave Guatemala in 1979, and went to live in exile in France. The poem 'XX' was published posthumously in a magazine in Guatemala. Arce's poems caused such protest from right-wing political leaders, particularly from the Movement of National Liberation, that the magazine in which they were published was suspended.

XX

'No, it's not him.'
'Yes, it is him.'
'No, it's not him. It's not possible, that this could be him.'
'Look, the scar from the injection.'
'No, it's not him.'
'Look, the crowned tooth which Miguel fixed for him six
    months ago.'
'No, it's not him.'
'I think that it is him, that this time it is him.'
'No, it's not him.'
How could it be him if he's got no eyes.
How could it be him if he's lost his worker's hands.
How could it be him if they have cut his balls off.
How could it be him without his guitar and song,
without that frown of his
in moments of danger, without his smile at work,
without his voice mouthing his thoughts,
without that silly way of his when he used to give me flowers.
How could it be him.

It's not him, I tell you it's not him.
I don't want it to be him.

Let's just say for example
that this afternoon
Italy has won the World Cup.
People pour into the hot summer streets singing
and waving flags
in wild jubilation.
Let's say, for example, that they're happy;
their explosive happiness,
their mass party
brings them together.
Each and every Italian scored all the goals on the pitch.
Let's say, for example, that I've seen a tiny Japanese man
swimming amongst the festive crowd
with a flag
dancing, jumping, shouting
in support of Italy in Tokyo Japanese.
And let's say that I,
who was a fan of Pepino Toledo,
of Gigante Rodriguez,
of Mito Marroquin and of Tarzan Segura,
who sold my bed as a boy
to get into the Municipal-Saprissa game
and played on the wing and in defence
when I was young,
am standing on a corner in Florence or Rome
watching a happy people
and that I can't forget
the massacres in my country.

Anonymous

This poem was circulated in Burma in 1991, at the time of the death in prison of Maung Thawka, a poet and democracy activist.

Quite unfair and cruel to boot

I have never heard
That a whole abdomen had to be opened up
Just to cure a mild case of diarrhoea.
I have never heard
That an entire pile of books was burnt
Just because a single termite blighted one.
I have never heard
That a spoilt child was stabbed
Just to scold him for crying for sweets.
I have never heard
That death sentences have been handed down
To minor violators of the Highway Code.
But I have heard that
The odious sentence of a lifetime's transportation
Has been given
For one small offence of rightly being angry
For just one day.

Nadezhda Mandelstam

Nadezhda Mandelstam (1899–1980) wrote some of the finest prose witnessing the terror of Stalin's Soviet Union. Her husband Osip was arrested several times for 'writing anti-Soviet poems' and spent long periods in prison for counter-revolutionary activity. He is thought to have died in 1938 near Vladivostok in a transit camp, on his way to prison. He was already dead when this letter was sent.

Last Letter   22 October 1938

Osia, my beloved, faraway sweetheart!

I have no words, my darling, to write this letter that you may never read, perhaps. I am writing it into empty space. Perhaps you will come back and not find me here. Then this will be all you have left to remember me by.

Osia, what a joy it was living together like children – all our squabbles and arguments, the games we played, and our love. Now I do not even look at the sky. If I see a cloud, who can I show it to?

Remember the way we brought back provisions to make our poor feasts in all the places where we pitched our tent like nomads? Remember the good taste of bread when we got it by a miracle and ate it together? And our last winter in Voronezh. Our happy poverty, and the poetry you wrote. I remember the time we were coming back once from the baths, when we bought some eggs or sausage, and a cart went by loaded with hay. It was still cold and I was freezing in my short jacket (but nothing like what we must suffer now: I know how cold you are). That day comes back to me now. I understand so clearly, and ache from the pain of it, that those winter days with all their troubles were the greatest and last happiness to be granted us in life.

My every thought is about you. My every tear and every smile is for you. I bless every day and every hour of our

16

bitter life together, my sweetheart, my companion, my blind guide in life.

Like two blind puppies we were, nuzzling each other and feeling so good together. And how fevered your poor head was, and how madly we frittered away the days of our life. What joy it was, and how we always knew what joy it was.

Life can last so long. How hard and long for each of us to die alone. Can this fate be for us who are so inseparable? Puppies and children, did we deserve this? Did you deserve this, my angel? Everything goes on as before. I know nothing. Yet I know everything – each day and hour of your life are plain and clear to me as in a delirium.

You came to me every night in my sleep, and I kept asking what had happened, but you did not reply.

In my last dream I was buying food for you in a filthy hotel restaurant. The people with me were total strangers. When I had bought it, I realised I did not know where to take it, because I do not know where you are.

When I woke up, I said to Shura: 'Osia is dead.' I do not know whether you are still alive, but from the time of that dream, I have lost track of you. I do not know where you are. Will you hear me? Do you know how much I love you? I could never tell you how much I love you. I cannot tell you even now. I speak only to you, only to you. You are with me always, and I who was such a wild and angry one and never learned to weep simple tears – now I weep and weep and weep.

It's me: Nadia. Where are you?

Farewell.

Nadia.

Translated by Max Hayward

Ayshe Yanar

Ayshe Yanar is an ex-client of the Foundation. She is a Kurd from Turkey who was tortured. She remarried, had a baby and is presumed to be still living in exile. We have not been able to contact her and we would very much like to hear from her.

Extract from *Quatrain*

Dark eyes dive again
into the distance.
The past burns our hearts.
We were forced into a trap.

Darkness before sunset.
My God,
either make this life easier
or forget about creating your servant.

One after the other my hopes
have been rubbed out and gone.
My dreams like flowers
have withered and perished.

Now pains, worries, aches
have taken the place of happiness.
My good friend is my enemy,
I have lost my tomorrow.

So the sun never rises,
the sea has no waves.
A star shot in my dream, tangled my hair
and took my youth away.

Translated by Richard McKane

Wei Jingsheng

Wei Jingsheng (born 1950), a former Red Guard, was working as an electrician in the Beijing Zoo in 1978 when he became a leader in the Democracy Wall Movement. An outspoken critic of government policy and advocate of individual rights since then, he was imprisoned in China from 1979 to 1993. Rearrested and imprisoned again in early 1994, he was given a fourteen-year sentence. He was released in 1997 on the condition that he went into exile. He now lives in the USA.

'Dear Prison Warden Xing'
Extract from *The Courage to Stand Alone*

16 March 1982

Dear Prison Warden Xing,

There are several small matters that I probably shouldn't bother you with, but it seems that I must. I'm not entirely to blame for these and there's no real need for blame at all, but things are already such that I still had better discuss them with you.

I haven't been sleeping well for quite some time now. There are several reasons for this, but the main thing preventing me from getting a sound night's sleep is the light that shines in my eyes all night long. My principle is: if I can make do, then I won't bother the people who work here. I know that work of any kind is not easy, and all jobs have their difficulties. That's why I went ahead and fashioned the aluminium foil from a few packs of cigarettes into a shade in order to block out some of the bright light that is reflecting off the ceiling and into my eyes.

But who would have known that not only was this prohibited, when I tried to explain that it wasn't interfering with anyone's work, I was scolded for 'not understanding reason'. No one explained to me why the shade was prohibited and it was even inferred that I was too young to make such trouble. This left me at a complete loss. I feel that even in prisons today, all actions should be explained. Saying there is 'no need to explain' to those who don't understand your reasons, and explaining things only to those who do, is a bit unreasonable in itself, wouldn't you say?

I would like to request that you pay some attention to this matter. It's not that the others' words are so unbearable – everyone in prison knows how to listen, after all – but because they can't always say things so directly. I've thought about writing you before this because my health and spirit can no longer take the prolonged lack of sleep and the depression I feel from staying in this tiny cell and never seeing the light of day. I heard that when Wang Guangmei was in prison (not here, of course) she lost her mind for the same reasons. Although this has been openly denied by some, I still believe the 'rumours' coming from people close to her are more reliable than the lying newspapers. Besides, there is no longer any reason to cover up for actions taken by the Gang of Four. Things are much different now and I don't want to be the first to follow in Wang Guangmei's footsteps, no matter what. I don't feel that asking to have the light turned off at night and going outside for some sun and exercise now and then with the brigade leader's permission can be considered unreasonable requests.

As far as I can tell, filling such requests does not constitute 'special treatment' here. In the cell next to mine and all the others I can see outside my door and window, the lights are off at night. Besides, I haven't gotten into any fights and I'm not plotting an escape, so isn't the fact that I have been locked up in the strict-regime brigade for so long 'special' treatment enough? I asked unsuccessfully to be dealt with in the same manner as political prisoners connected to the Gang of Four, but I was sent here just the same. Why, then, can't I at least be treated like an ordinary political prisoner? I don't understand why I should receive special punishment, for even if someone is abusing public power to retaliate against me, there is no enmity between you and me, so can't we find a way to talk this over? If this is not something controlled by the higher-ups, then I would like to ask you, Secretary Zhao, Political Instructor Chen and Brigade Leader Zhao to contemplate my request in a timely fashion. I also hope that this request will not interfere with my family visits, because today, for some unknown reason, I was not allowed to see them.

Wei Jingsheng

Translated by Kristina M. Torgeson

Alfredo Cordal

Alfredo Cordal (born 1941) worked as a journalist in Chile in charge of a magazine for the workers in the factories along the coast of the country. He also worked as a freelance journalist covering cultural news in the Press Department of Channel 13 Catholic University. At the time of the military coup in September 1973, he was suspended from work and underwent interrogation by the military for five months. In February 1974, he managed to get to Buenos Aires, Argentina, where he was treated for acute paranoia, together with other Chilean friends. Many of the psychologists and Argentine friends who helped at that time are still missing. He came to the UK as a refugee in 1974, before the coup in Argentina in 1975. He now lives in London and works as a journalist and Spanish teacher. He has been writing plays and poems and doing readings of his poetry for Amnesty International, Praxis and other human-rights organizations.

Walk

This dog always pulls us in a hurry
following up the invisible track of forgotten times,
with its neck tense, the mouth pointing forward and low
it's dragging us to a row of graves
under the shadows of St Mark's churchyard.
And we discover names and dates
almost erased on the stone graves:
'Thomas W . . . is . . . John Prest . . . Mary 1 . . . 8 . . . 3
Elisabeth . . . An . . . 1 . . . 7 . . . 4 . . . Horatio Oliver . . . '
and the names almost erased of 'Henry Albin . . . Amy
    Tidey . . .
Louise . . . ' children names of parents' already erased
    names,
all under the same indelible words:
'To the memory of . . . '
And looking at the top of a big tree

we can see also our name almost erased
from the memory of this changeable sky.
And a blow of cold wind wipes out our smile among the
    leaves,
because we know that if this faithful dog
were to be in other lands
it could not keep following the track
of so many names never erased,
never written, neither read nor meant
on stone graves, never ever erected.

Translated by Alfredo Cordal and Seth Sethna

Miguel Hezo Mixco

Miguel Hezo Mixco was in 1991 a combatant in the El Salvadoran Frente Martí de Liberacion Nacional.

If Death . . .

If death should come asking for me
do me the favour
of telling him to come back tomorrow
because I still haven't paid my debts
nor finished a poem
nor said goodbye to anyone
nor prepared clothing for the trip
nor delivered that package I promised to
nor locked up my desk drawers
nor told my friends what I should have
nor sniffed the fragrance of the unborn rose
nor laid bare my roots
nor answered an overdue letter
because I haven't even washed my hands
or known a son
or gone hiking in unknown countries
nor do I know the sea's seven sails
nor the song of mariners
If death should come
please tell him I understand
and to wait a bit
because I haven't kissed my sweetheart goodbye
nor shaken hands with my family
nor dusted my books
nor whistled my favourite song
nor become reconciled with my enemies
tell him I haven't yet attempted suicide
nor seen my people freed
tell him if he comes to return tomorrow

that it's not because I fear him but because
I haven't even set off along the road.

Translated by Claribel Alegría and Darwin J. Flakoll

Wanjiku

Wanjiku (Chorn 1957), a Kikuyu woman from Kenya, comes from a family that spent years in active opposition to President Daniel arap Moi, singing and recording songs and producing leaflets critical of his corrupt and oppressive rule. Today, her parents and four of her brothers are dead, killed because of their activities. Wanjiku, now hiding in exile, walks with difficulty because of the police torture she endured.

Testimony

I had a farm, a husband, my own business, a house and a family. It was a very good life. I was very comfortable. Now almost everything I had is gone. But politics is like a disease. Once you catch it, it stays with you. I couldn't stand by and watch what was happening without speaking out – there was corruption everywhere.

We were members of FORD-Asili [Forum for the Restoration of Democracy]. We used to record songs in Kikuyu, and distribute the tapes at rallies. The Kikuyu are the largest tribe in Kenya but Moi keeps them from any power.

My husband was the first to go. He worked for an opposition paper. When he didn't return from a trip outside Nairobi, we feared the worst. That's what you do there when people disappear. He turned up a week later in the mortuary, allegedly the victim of a car accident, but the circumstances were very suspicious.

Then my parents were killed. The police tried to say it was a gas explosion in their home but the bodies had been hacked and there were political slogans on the walls.

Two of my other brothers were then shot, one was stabbed to death and one died in prison after being caught with banned publications. Then they came for me, a few months before the general election in December 1992.

I had a shop where I sold clothes at the front. At the back we produced the songs and pamphlets. Somehow they traced the address from a rally where our music had been played and I was arrested. After they took me away they burned the building down.

I was taken to Nyati, a well-known interrogation house in Nairobi, where as soon as I entered, I was pushed down some steps. I was handcuffed and fell very badly. My spine has been weak since I was a child and this made things very bad. The nerves were damaged and since then it has been difficult to walk.

They picked me up then, and threw me into a cell where the conditions were disgusting. There was water on the floor several inches deep – water and faeces – which I had to lie in. I couldn't stand because of my injuries.

That night two officers took me from the cell to another room. They raped me and they sodomized me. They put burning cigarettes on my bottom and chilli powder inside me. I don't know how long it went on because I lost consciousness. Afterwards they put me back in the cell but I remained unconscious and eventually woke up in hospital.

I stayed in hospital a long time. Then, when I went home, I started helping the movement again. I couldn't help myself. Like I said, politics is a disease. So in January 1995 the police came for me again. They ransacked my house, found some more pamphlets and took me off to jail, where they kept me three months.

Things were very bad for me. I had to sleep on the floor because of my back. It seemed there was no way out until an officer from my own tribe started working there and I was able to sell some land and bribe him to release me.

I then came to Britain to try to find my daughter who had fled abroad with another of my brothers. I was overjoyed to find her but inside I felt I had nothing to live for. I was on the point of giving up. After all I had been through, I was very depressed.

At the beginning, I cried whenever I talked about my torture, but with counselling at the Medical Foundation for

the Care of Victims of Torture I have been better able to
handle the experience. Talking about it in a women's group
with other people who have been through similar
experiences was also very helpful. It was staff at the Medical
Foundation who persuaded me to fight on. They made me
realize that if I didn't, my abusers would have won.

IDENTITY

The sense of self comes under threat.

Babek

I became a teacher when I was seventeen years old and moved out from the town to a small village. The people I met there helped me to understand myself. There was great poverty there but the people and the village gave me so much. They gave me a sense of identity as I understood what I could do for them. I learned that I wasn't there just to teach them A and B but another alphabet. We each had a gift for one another. I felt I had a responsibility for them – I had been educated and compared to them I was privileged.

When my students, some as young as ten, were being sent away to fight in the war, I felt that I had to stand up for them. And that was why I was taken away. Sometimes during interrogation, that sense of identity and why I was there did not feel so strong. I thought to myself, Who am I to talk about people's rights? But then I realized that my interrogators were trying to steal something from me and I thought that I didn't have to let them.

Erich Fried

Erich Fried (1921–1988) was born in Vienna. He fled Austria in 1938 after his father had been killed by the Gestapo; he came to live in London, where he tried to help others escape. After World War II, he worked in the German service of the BBC. His work became popular in Germany in the 1960s and he often travelled there to give readings. His political and love poems became best sellers. He translated the works of Shakespeare, Dylan Thomas and Sylvia Plath.

In Hiding

I must learn to hide
from my persecutors
and am thereby
in double danger

Perhaps still not well enough
hidden from them
and perhaps by now
hidden too well from myself

Translated by Stuart Hood

Tsuboi Shigeji

Tsuboi Shigeji (1889–1975) was a founder of the Japan Proletarian Winter's League journal *Red and Black*. As a member of the league, he was twice imprisoned for his leftist position.

Silent but . . .

I may be silent, but
I'm thinking.
I may not talk, but
Don't mistake me for a wall.

Translated by Geoffrey Bownan and Anthony Thwaite

Brian Keenan

Brian Keenan was born in Belfast in 1950. He completed a degree in English literature at the Coleraine University, then went on to work in Brussels and Spain. He returned to Ireland and taught in his old school and later worked in community-development centres across Belfast. He then went on to take an MA in Anglo-Irish literature and an adult-education course. He went to work in Beirut University in 1985. It was while he was there that he was kidnapped by fundamentalist Shi'ite militiamen and held in the suburbs of Beirut for the next four and a half years. For much of that time he was on his own; he was later held with other hostages, including John McCarthy. He now lives in Ireland, writes and lectures at Trinity College.

Extract from *An Evil Cradling*

My thoughts were frequently occupied by the loss of my humanity. What had I become? What had I descended to as I sat here in my corner? I walked the floor day after day, losing all sense of the man I had been, in half-trances recognizing nothing of myself. Was I a kind of Kafkaesque character transformed out of human form into some animal, something to be shunned and locked away from the world?

In my creature-condition, for hours I would question myself about the differences between the wild and the tame. A wild animal lives in a constant state of awareness and readiness. It must decide for itself. A domestic creature makes no decisions. I thought it must be like this with the soul. It is always ready for life, choosing and deciding and instinctively creating life. The wild are more fearless than courageous. Their instinct is to be constantly mobile, in a state of readiness to face the unexpected. The untamed soul is exclusively interested in simply being. It has no desire to sit in quiet contemplation of the world. I thought of animals in the zoo, with their desperate patience or spirit beguiled into some neurotic state pacing to and fro, their minds empty.

I began to understand why it is that so many creatures in captivity will not mate. And with it I began to understand my own rage at my impotence, at the powerlessness of my flesh. Perhaps the power of love is only meaningful in freedom. Such thoughts were frequently interrupted by panic. Time was taken from me. How long, how long would I be here? Would my period here, however long it was, erode from me that capacity to indulge and to be fully engaged in life? I would think back on those moments of insanity, all those strange and fantastic places to which the mind took me, running after it or being dragged behind it. And I began to see the awful limitation of one lifetime.

Maria Jastrzebska

This poem appeared in a magazine called *GEN* (Issue 12/13: Refugee Women in Britain) which is no longer published. We were unable to find Maria Jastrzebska and would very much like to hear from her.

half poem

this is a half poem
for the half of my heart
which beats fast when I'm frightened
and for the other half
which is braver
beating loudly
brimming over with anger
or love

for my life which is forever falling apart
in half pieces
before it comes together again as a whole
for the way there is usually more than one truth
and often more than two halves
for the halves that don't come in half sizes

this is a half poem
for the half of me that is most unacceptable
least public
at any given time
and for that half of the population
who've always had
the biggest half of my heart

Ken Saro-Wiwa

Ken Saro-Wiwa (1941–1995) was one of Nigeria's best-known writers. He was a member of the Ogoni tribe, whose land has been exploited by multinational companies extracting oil. Ken Saro-Wiwa opposed this action and the military governments in power in Nigeria. He was arrested and charged with incitement to murder, and was executed by hanging on 10 November 1995.

Extract from *On the Death of Ken Saro-Wiwa*

The Task Force Commander knew his onions. He seized me from my bed at midnight, his men having broken into my house by force of arms. He had me beaten black and blue, then he manacled me and threw me into a torture chamber in a secret location with instruction that I must remain incommunicado and be stunned to death. For good measure, he took pictures of me in chains with both video and still cameras to show his masters that he was 'doing his job', so he said through the lenses. And I have it on good authority that the images were and still are a great source of joy to Lt-Col Komo. He shows them till date to his family, to visitors and to the public as evidence of his great success as an officer and a gentleman trained, for God's sake, in Sandhurst and Georgetown University. Give a good thing to an African and he'll spoil it!

Physical torture did not kill me. Nor did mental torture. Then, one night, the ghost arrived. Tall and gangly, dressed in ragged Nigerian Army camouflage uniform, his bones shooting out of holes in the uniform, his brown teeth as huge as tusks projecting from enormous lips, he came to me, automatic weapon slung over his shoulder, a little drum, an Ogoni drum called 'Ekoni' in his hand. He sounded the drum, Ken-ti-mo, Ken-ti-mo, Ken-ti-mo!

The familiar sound of the little drum woke me up. At the sight of the ghost, I laughed. Annoyed by my laughter, he dropped the drum and laid hold of his automatic weapon. He pointed it at me at close range. I did not flinch. He cocked the weapon and fingered the trigger. I did not bat an eyelid.

'Who are you?' I asked.

'I'm General Jeno Saidu.'

'Sounds like genocide to me,' I said.

'You should know.'

'What do you want?' I asked.

'I'm here to finish you,' replied he, in a gruff voice.

'General, stop swaggering. You do not impress me.'

'You will be impressed. I've finished all your Ogoni people – men, women and children. Once I deal with you, my task is done.'

'Go ahead,' I challenged him.

'You are not afraid to die?'

'No.'

'Why not?'

'I'm prepared to go up with all my people whom you confess to having already murdered.'

'Yes, I worked hard on them. I made short work of them. All five hundred thousand of them. You are my last man.'

'So, go ahead.'

General Jeno Saidu, the ghost, shot into the ceiling. I laughed.

'Why did you shoot into the ceiling and not into my chest?'

'You're still not afraid?'

'No, General.'

'And why not?'

'Because I have what is greater than your weapon.' Whereupon I said, after the English poet Blake:

'I will not cease from mental fight
Nor shall my sword sleep in my hand
Till we have built a new Ogoni
In Niger delta's wealthy land.'

Then I drew my pen from under my pillow. The general's

weapon fell from his hand, his tusks from his mouth and he slumped to his knee.

Yes, the moment I drew my pen from under my pillow General Jeno Saidu became as meek as a lamb. He lost his swagger which I thought he would, and became my confidence. From which I drew the lesson, if I did know it beforehand, that these Generals are strong only if they have an automatic weapon in their hands. Without that, they are as dumb as pap and sit much the same where you place them and will then become civil and human.

General Jeno Saidu, ghost as he was, asked me to sheathe my pen and he would tell me a thing or two about my torture and the death he had inflicted on Ogoni men, women and children.

I put my pen back underneath my pillow. The ghost sighed with relief and made a seat for himself beside me on the bed. He reeked of human blood and I had to hold up my nose.

'Sorry about the smell,' says he. 'There's nothing I can do about it. All the soap in the world, all the deodorants in the market will not wash it off me. I've murdered too many Ogoni people in the past month. I don't mean to hurt you, Ken, if I may call you by that endearing name which all my victims cried as they went to their death. No, I don't mean to hurt you. I did what I did on orders. Orders is orders, I must tell you. Even as a General, orders is orders. I tell the truth.

'I was told to shoot into the air, drive your people into the forest, the bushes and marshes, dispose of them there to destroy all evidence of death, then return to their rickety towns and burn as many of them down as I could. Thereafter, I was to visit my power on all goats, chickens, yams and plantains. That, my dear Ken, is what we call a scorched earth policy.

'I did what I had to do, man. Orders is orders. My last task was to come and finish you off. I confess that I missed my way coming to the secret location where you are held. The description given to me was not exact. I went past the Imo River and crossing a river always has a dampening effect on me. It forces me to think, for a while at least. And it was no different this night.

'And you know, I realized that in all those villages we went to, there was not a single gun. I mean, it's really sweet to annihilate a powerful enemy, or one who at least answers you back. But to be ordered to annihilate babies and pregnant mothers sleeping in their beds. That is madness. And what is it that can make anyone so mad?

'In Nigeria, it is money. Your country is money-mad, Ken. There is nothing people will not do for money. And you who sit on rich deposits of oil and gas are doomed. I hear the famous jingle "We are one" on your Radio Rivers every day. And I laugh to think anyone believes it. You know, we soldiers, we use deception as a tool of war. So all propaganda. So we organize prayers for peace while we murder, loot and burn. We are after the oil and gas, Ken. And anything above that oil which lies in the depth of the land is due for extermination.

'And don't think we are the only ones who need the money. The Europeans and Americans need it even more. And after all, they are the ones whose brains and money bring the oil and gas from the earth to the surface. They are the ones who buy the oil and gas and then pay you some money. Their only friend is he who allows them to take the oil away as cheaply as possible. Therefore, a man like you, Ken, who dares to ask them to pay a bit more money, take care of the people on the land, put back something, wash their trousers or whatever, you are a mortuary candidate. Worms' meat.

'I have to tell you the truth. I go all over this country unseen. I am General Jeno Saidu. Unless I reveal myself, you never know. But I am in all councils of dangerous men to take orders. I know the origin of your present ordeal.

'No, don't speak. You know those in-laws and friends of yours who met their sad end a month or so ago. They suffered a fate that was meant for you. You should have died shortly after at that same spot. But you are a lucky man. You probably have a mission. That bag of bones they took to Government House. That man who told the world that you incited the youths, whereas you were in your car all the way under escort and spoke to no one till you got to Port Harcourt long before I and my men did what we were ordered to do, that man, I say, is a paid agent. And he was well rehearsed to say all he said. I think we will still have to invent more lies if you do not die by torture.

'As to your present ordeal, the origin lies in that gas pipeline which is supposed to go through the heart of Ogoni to the German aluminium smelter plant in Akwa Ihom State. You remember that guy from the Italian company Saipen who tried to offer you inducement for you to allow them to start constructing the pipeline? And you know Shell has already awarded a $500 million contract to those who are to design a pipeline to deliver the gas which they believe is theirs. You dared, through MOSOP, to ask the Ogoni people to resist the construction of the pipeline until an environmental impact assessment study has been completed to determine what harm the pipeline would do to the Ogoni people.

'Environmental impact studies are only good for white people in their country. The headquarters of the three companies I have mentioned have asked their employees in Nigeria why the project is being delayed. And the answer is Ken Saro-Wiwa and MOSOP. These impediments have to be removed and any other Ogoni people who stand in the way. I swear to you, that is the game plan. I know. I was sat at the meeting where the decisions were taken. And I have my orders.

'And if you do not believe me, if you do not believe the torture through which you have been put, the denial to you of medical treatment, of a lawyer's attention, of your family's love, if you do not believe the chains on your legs, then wait until they take you for interrogation. If the detective is not the same man who detects what he is asked to detect, then you can give me up. But before you do so, write your story.

Write it fast.

Goodbye.'

He spoke and disappeared as only a ghost can and I woke up with a start from my sleep. The rest of the story you already know.

Ediba-Bakira Kapic

I was born in Stolac, Bosnia and Herzegovina, in 1976 and I lived there for sixteen years. I was in Stolac for the first five months of war in 1992, and then I went to Croatia to live there as a refugee. My mother joined me there later, but my father stayed in Stolac, because he wanted to and because he is an orthopaedic surgeon, and he was needed. My father was imprisoned by Croats in 1993 and was kept in various concentration camps for thirteen months. During this period, I had come to London, as the Croats did not want me in their country and didn't allow me to go to school as I am a Muslim. When I came to London, I missed my family so much, especially my dad, whom I didn't know anything about, so I wrote a poem. I have two brothers, and they are both in Sarajevo, and so are my mum and dad now. I am doing physics, chemistry and maths A level.

Ediba returned to join her family in September 1996. They have not been able to return to their home town. She is now studying for a degree in English and English literature.

Father

Somewhere in the back there is a picture
a picture of somebody long time forgotten
of somebody who I don't know any more
somebody who lives the life of dreams,
somebody who is not me any more.
And as the pictures go by, like
the sad movie with a story that
brings tears
I remember
a hug, a smile, pockets full of love
past life
The newborn dreams with fear of waking up
feels the reality pressed hard on the skin

opens the eyes with a wish of not seeing.
The new one lives the life of nightmares.
So strong while so gentle it comes
the little thing turns your day
a penny of love from his pocket
filled with nice-smelling tobacco
Hardly given but holds more than
thousand others
a hug takes your face on the shirt with
a smell of the loved one who washed it
While the pipe rests in his hands,
the lips make a move and a heart jumped with pride
'cause it's only for her
hiding all the unnecessary words
smile – enough to tell on its own
the story of love
somebody who used to be me
somebody who let the life make her forget
somebody who is hiding a child deep inside
somebody who remembers a father

Chantal

Chantal, born in 1976, is a Tutsi survivor of the genocide in Rwanda.

Testimony

The genocide changed my personality and my way of thinking. It changed everything for me. I don't trust people at all. In Rwanda before the genocide our neighbours were very friendly. They came to us every single day – when we had a party we invited them, when the woman was having a baby, my father drove her to hospital. But it's them who killed my family, it's them who made the genocide.

As children we were confused. We knew that in school some teachers and kids were racist but our parents wouldn't tell us why there was so much anger. When I asked, my father told me that I would find out when I was older. I was brilliant at school but when I was twelve I didn't get my exam to go to secondary school. That's when I realized something was going on.

When you take your exams, if you are a Tutsi you can't win. You can't stay in a public school because of orders from the Hutu rulers. You have to go to a private one. My sister didn't win as well. We wanted to go to a state school. It was cheaper and the materials were better but we didn't qualify. I was crying and my dad told me I had to realize that life was like that. He was in school but didn't get a diploma. His relatives didn't go to school.

When my dad told me I was very curious to learn why this was happening to my tribe. I wanted to find out how grandfather lived. The Hutus said the Tutsis had killed them, so I tried to find out more in books in the museum and library. They were in French, most of them written by priests, but I couldn't find anything that explained things properly.

In 1990 the Rwandan Patriotic Liberation Front became

more active and the government wanted to mobilize the population against them, saying it was a Tutsi organization although really it was mixed. There were Hutus in it as well. The government lied to the people and accused educated Tutsis in Rwanda of helping the RPLF and began to beat them up, kill them. They put thousands in Nyamirambo Stadium in Kigali near where I lived. They were kept a week without drink or food, until people started to eat grass. About 20,000 people died inside.

My mum, a schoolteacher who taught French and Kirwanda, used to tell me about her father who was killed by Hutu soldiers in 1959, but to me it was just a story. Then the soldiers came for her and my father. She was in her night clothes, with no shoes on, when they came to the house. They had big black plastic whips and they beat her up, then took her to Prison 1930 in Kigali. My dad was outside the country and my older sister was at boarding school so I was the oldest in the house, looking after my younger brothers and sisters.

They let her go after about six months and my dad came back and things kept getting worse. In 1992 a lot of Tutsis living in Gisenji were exterminated. Some said as many as 50,000 died, all killed with machetes. Then they started to kill Tutsi children at boarding schools. My family became very worried.

In January 1994 the killings really started in Kigali and on 6 April the government declared openly that Hutus should kill Tutsis. Don't ask me to talk about the genocide . . . There are things I will never tell anyone.

War is mad, crazy, it makes you crazy as well. Imagine someone comes and kills your sisters and kills your mother and father behind you. You're afraid. All you can think about is whether in a minute it will be your turn to die.

My father and my little sister were shot in front of me. My other sister and two brothers were also shot. My mother and I hid with a cousin, then after my father was buried we left the area because the Interahamwe [Hutu extremists] wanted to rape all the Tutsi girls.

A Jehovah's Witness friend who was a Hutu tried to save me by hiding me at his house, but the Interahamwe armed with clubs came looking for me. They took me into the bush to kill me. I was there with a mother and her child. They started shooting at us and I fell into a pit full of corpses. I was wounded but after the Hutus left I managed to climb out.

I hid for a while in Kigali, then made for another town, Kibuye, where things were hardly any better, and in the end I was forced to hide in the forest. I had always been terrified of the bush when I was in Kigali but I knew it was my only chance. It was there that I was found by the French Army who looked after me.

Now I don't think there is a future for victims of genocide in Rwanda. Take a woman in Rwanda who used to have seven children – one day she wakes up and all these seven have been killed. And you know the people who killed them, they are her neighbours. No justice for them. Who cares? You just see your neighbours come and say good morning to you and you know they killed your children. How do you feel? Do you think you have hope? Do you think you have a future?

I was going to study electronics. I was good at it and my father encouraged me, but now that's all gone. In my country we have this culture, even when you are hungry you are not supposed to tell anyone you're hungry. You light a fire and put on a saucepan of water so no one knows. You just try to be smart, wear nice clothes and show people you are happy when inside you are dead already. So that's what I'm doing now.

I'm a refugee. I have just one brother and one cousin left living in Kigali. I want them to join me – I need a family to remind me who I am, what life could have been like. But my brother is eighteen and the British government won't let him come to London. He looks after my cousin who is fourteen. So I don't know what will happen now. I just hope that God remembers me soon because he has forgotten me for a very long time.

IMPACT

The effect of torture and repression do not remain in a prison cell. Friends and family suffer too. The fabric of society cannot stay the same.

Babek

When a country is like ours, where there is torture and repression, it has an impact on everyone. People are not free in my country, there is a shadow of terror. You are living in a worried society. Since this government came to power, you worry about everything. I was taken out of society and put in prison but the whole country is in a cage. The bigger prison is my country.

Everyone has their story. Everyone has lost at least one person – they may have died in prison or they may have died in the war.

This regime has created fear and killed trust in people's minds and hearts, they have destroyed it. And once that is lost you cannot really bring it back. Relationships are changed.

When I came out of prison, there were people who used to be my friends who didn't want to be seen on the street with me. I had one friend and he used to take me to the cemeteries to walk. I said to him, 'I suffered for you and now you can't speak to me.' I was betrayed.

When I was released and I was not allowed to work as a teacher, I tried to work in any job I could find. I began to work as a taxi driver for a friend. But he came to me and said that I would have to leave. The authorities had threatened to explode his cab if he employed me. There were tears in his eyes but he could not let me work for him.

That is the impact.

Ariel Dorfman

Ariel Dorfman (born 1942), citizen of Chile and supporter of Salvador Allende, was forced into exile in 1973. He now lives mostly in the USA, where he teaches, and is considered to be a major critic. He is best known for his novels and the play *Death and the Maiden*, which deals with torture. He also wrote a moving collection of poems, *Last Waltz in Santiago*, dedicated to the 2,500 of his compatriots estimated to have gone missing during the Pinochet dictatorship.

Hope
for Edgardo Enriquez, Sr
for Edgardo Enriquez, Jr

My son has been
missing
since May 8
of last year.

> They took him
> just for a few hours
> they said
> just for some routine
> questioning.

After the car left,
the car with no licence plate,
we couldn't

> find out

anything else
about him.

But now things have changed.
We heard from a compañero
who just got out
that five months later

they were torturing him
in Villa Grimaldi,
at the end of September
they were questioning him
in the red house
that belonged to the Grimaldis.

They say they recognized
his voice his screams
they say.

Somebody tell me frankly
what times are these
what kind of world
what country?
What I'm asking is
how can it be
that a father's
joy
a mother's
joy
is knowing
that they
that they are still
torturing
their son?
Which means
that he was alive
five months later
and our greatest
hope
will be to find out
next year
that they're still torturing him
eight months later

and he may might could
still be alive.

Primo Levi

Primo Levi (1919–1987) was born in Turin, Italy. As a young man, at the time of the persecution of the Italian Jews, he joined a band of partisans but was soon captured, and in 1944 he was sent to the Auschwitz concentration camp, where his training as a chemist helped him to survive. He wrote an extraordinary account of the experience of the death camps, *If This Is a Man*, and won many prizes for his prose and fiction. But in his later years he became increasingly depressed and he fell to his death, almost certainly by suicide, from the stairwell of his home in 1987.

Thieves

They come at night, like wisps of fog.
Often in full daylight too.
Unnoticed, they filter through
Cracks and keyholes,
Noiselessly, leaving no trace,
No broken locks, and no disorder.
They are the thieves of time,
Fluid and sticky like leeches:
They drink your time and spit it out
The way you'd toss away trash.
You've never seen them face to face. Do they have faces?
Lips and tongue – yes, certainly
And tiny pointed teeth.
They suck without provoking pain,
Leave only a livid scar.

14 October 1995

Translated by Ruth Feldman and Brian Swann

In the following piece, all the names were changed to protect people's identities. 'Mourad', in his sixties, is a former Algerian rebel who fought the French.

Mourad

Letters from Algeria

8 October 1994

Hello, Old Pal,

Still another unsigned letter. Pretty cowardly, I admit! But those bastards are still sorting the mail in many of the post offices. Algiers is being drained. Algiers is almost empty. So many of those bastards have run away! Not so long ago, they were strutting along the corridors of power, gallivanting around the world at the people's expense. Today, like rats, they are the first to abandon the sinking ship. You can bet your life they are posing as good democrats, now that they live in the shadow of the Eiffel Tower!

Fear! What a vile word! Death! But what can we do? Yes, I am afraid, afraid of having my throat slit, afraid of having my brains blown out. I am afraid for my sons, for my daughter, for my wife, for myself, for my brothers and their children. I am even afraid of my shadow, of a glance from somebody I don't know, of the mere presence of a stranger, of the telephone ringing, of a knock at the door, of roadblocks, of cars that are just behind me, or pass by when I am at the market, going to buy cigarettes or simply walking down the street.

And when night falls! Then it's insomnia! At the slightest sound, I leap out of bed. Thursday, in the centre of town, five policemen were gunned down as they sat in their car in front of a lycée. The day before yesterday, a teacher at

Nôtre-Dame-d'Afrique was murdered. Two weeks ago, a neighbour, three other men and a young girl had their throats cut. Not to speak of the slaughter of entire families, the shooting of the elderly, the abduction and rape of girls and women, the burning of buildings, the closing of schools ... It is SHEER HORROR. I hesitated a long time before writing, because the only thing I can tell you about is our bloody Hell.

Give my love to Natalie and Christine.

Mourad

15 July 1995

My dear Jean,

How are you? How is your health? I have been down in the dumps lately. So I have not written. It is so hard just to 'survive'. Not only do we have to put up with the terrorist attacks, but with the terrorism of the International Monetary Fund as well. Every day, the prices of certain products change, go up, of course. It's crazy! Some people are getting rich overnight, while misery spreads. Until recently, we always ate yogurt. The price has become prohibitive, so we've stopped. I used to buy two pairs of trousers a year. Now I can hardly afford to buy even one. When the doctor gives you a prescription, you can only get one or two out of the five or six items prescribed. We have 1,200 kilometres of coastline and fish has become a luxury. As for fruit: only on paydays!

Best regards to Natalie and Christine.

Your old Pal

1 September 1995

Hello Old Pal,

Your letter was not too much of a surprise, especially since it took a month to get here and arrived sellotaped ...

No part of the country can now be considered safe. People avoid going out any more than is absolutely necessary. They go to work and then home again. And that is already quite an accomplishment. Because there are now car bombs in the towns, explosives on the roads, derailed trains . . .

Since life must go on, we have to leave the house from time to time, always aware that death may be waiting just around the corner or else may come to call on us in our homes and even . . . in the mosques, in the midst of our prayers.

So, I should tell you that in the face of this 'national terror', for several months we've had what is called '*les gardes communaux*', or the local guard. Each village or town 'hires' these guards who must be residents. Many are veterans of the Algerian War, but most are recruited among the young. They are armed, they protect their town or village, and help the army and gendarmerie. As far as I know, they are effective. But the problem remains: just who are the people behind the terror??? Up to now, except for the former Prime Minister, Kasdi Merbah, and a few other officials, those responsible for the decline of this country have not been touched. What a paradox! I could go on for ever. But already the picture is black enough already. So, good-bye for now.

Your brother,
Mourad

29 March 1996

Hello,

The terrorists' latest actions have been devastating. But the general feeling is that by the summer things will be much better. Many people think that the army is now in control. If so, long may it stay so!

Since Zeroual's election, the situation is clearer: the army supports the majority of the population. You wrote that we are a long way from being a state of law. I agree with you.

Just after the Revolution, we thought we were in a state of law, but were immediately subjected to a dictatorship. We have been waiting patiently and are now nearing the end of our lives. Nothing has changed. The betrayal of the ideals for which our brothers died was and is so enormous, so unspeakable, that our generation will never live to see the state of law. The 'cataclysm' of another generation will be needed to remove the millstone of accumulated betrayals.

13 May 1996

Old Pal,

As we awake from our nightmare, we begin to take stock of the damages. What's more, our values have been turned upside down. It is more profitable to be a street hawker of illegally imported bric-à-brac than to be a university professor or engineer. Since there are no checks being made now – because officials say they need to concentrate on the anti-terrorist campaigns – large numbers of merchants no longer pay any taxes, others don't even bother with trade registers and you wouldn't believe the number of companies who declare bankruptcy after a lucrative operation. Pensions are delayed by ten days or more. You should see the crowds of people queuing up every day at the post office and coming out empty-handed with bowed heads. I have a confession to make: I am ashamed to say my pension no longer lasts until the end of the month! I have to borrow money to make ends meet!

19 June 1996

The descent into Hell continues inexorably. Life has become very hard. So hard that we forget that there is terrorism, that people are still dying violently every day. We forget that death lies in wait for us around every corner. We forget that one fine day we may leave the house never to return, or that one night, we may not live to see the dawn. We forget the army patrolling the streets, the masked guards standing in front of the schools, the armed policemen.

We have already forgotten the friends who have disappeared – murdered or gone into exile. We have forgotten that bookshops existed, that it was once possible to be admitted to any hospital at all for free care. We have forgotten the pride of citizenship (Algerian citizenship no less!). We have become like wildcats struggling to survive in the dry season. Oh yes, the market economy is indeed a wonderful thing. It means you can launder dirty money! And all of Algeria is being sold at a discount. Everything is up for sale, everything is being traded. The only thing left for the people is our poor old flag, witness to all the betrayals, all the robberies.

As the days pass, the great principles of fraternity, generosity, solidarity are being diluted to make way for the politics of profit, easy money and sleazy scheming.

What has happened to you, oh my Algeria?

Mourad

(Mourad's hopes, aroused by Liamine Zeroual's election to the Algerian presidency in November 1995, were tempered by the continuing economic difficulties and the persistent suspicion of corruption in high places.)

20 February 1997

Let me make one thing clear: the only ones who are protecting us against those monsters are the army and the security forces. There are monsters who have to be exterminated. That is the first step. Afterwards, we can discuss democracy and the rest. Life is very hard. I am crippled with debts. I can no longer eat what I would like to eat. I don't buy clothes any more. But I support the present government which is applying the diktat of the IMF and the World Bank.

5 March 1997

We no longer hear any talk about crimes or car bombs.
What is really going on? We've started asking questions.
Was the terrorism created to make possible the move to a
market economy? Because in normal times all these price
rises and bankruptcies would have sparked riots and led to
bloodbaths.

30 August 1997
(After the Rais massacre)

Today, I simply don't know what to write to you. I'll be so
happy to see the end of the 1990s!

Each day we are living with the horror of horrors. Given
the number of victims, the murderers must be an 'army'
and not just small groups. Cutting the throats of a hundred
people is quite a job! I once visited an abattoir and saw how
they cut the throats of sheep on a conveyor belt. It was total
pandemonium. With beef cattle and horses, it must be even
worse. But imagine human beings!

1 September 1997

Monday, one o'clock in the morning. A terrible storm. Then
gunshots and, from the mosque, four calls: 'Allah ou Akbar
[God is Great]', followed by 'Leave your houses at once!'

I had not yet fallen asleep. I heard voices in the street. I
went to the window, which was open, but the shutters were
closed and the lights out. There were more voices and
women's screams. My wife woke up and joined me. We
roused the children. There was no doubt. The terrorists, the
cut-throats, were coming. We dressed quickly and left the
house.

Once we were outside, neighbours took charge of my wife
and daughter. My eldest son and I joined the men in the

street. I was armed with a pitchfork, he with a hammer. All the wives and daughters from the immediate vicinity took refuge in a neighbour's house, whereas the men and boys, armed with axes, iron bars, knives and sticks, stood staunchly waiting for the cut-throats, ready to die in self-defence.

Three o'clock: three police cars sweep by like a whirlwind! Without stopping. The gendarmerie is only 200 meters from my house. They have four armoured vans parked on the sidewalk in front. But they have not moved.

Four o'clock: the police and the gendarmes we had seen go by, stop now beside us and tell us to go home. Somebody in the crowd answers, 'Give us your guns and you can go to bed.' Nobody paid any attention to the policemen's words.

Six o'clock: dawn breaks. The groups of ten to thirty persons separate and start back towards their homes: women, girls and boys, men, all barefoot, wearing only nightgowns, pyjamas, shorts or T-shirts. Fathers are carrying the babies.

At the sight of all these people who had left their beds so suddenly, without taking anything, not even their shoes, I was in tears. Where is the army? Where are the members of Parliament? Where is the state? Everybody is now demanding weapons. People have begun to understand that they must defend themselves, all ALONE, even without firearms. It's terrible. It's atrocious. It's unjust. It's utterly sickening.

Mourad

Collected by Philippe Bernard and Nathaniel Herzberg

María Eugenia Bravo Calderara

María Eugenia Bravo Calderara was born in Santiago, Chile, in 1940. At the time of the coup in 1973, she was a lecturer at the Universidad de Chile. She was taken to the National Stadium, tortured and imprisoned, but finally escaped to England in 1975. She has lived there ever since. Her first poems were kept by her mother, who buried them in her garden until later they were sent to Switzerland in a diplomatic bag. María Bravo was not able to visit her mother until 1990.

She has published her own volume of poetry and her work has appeared in magazines and anthologies. Love and exile and the memory of prison have been at the core of her poetry. As a literary critic, she is also the author of a book on Pablo Neruda's poetry.

The People of Orpheus

You may not know this: the ones
who have gone like Orpheus
down to the regions of hell,
have a bond between them, much
stronger than blood.

These people, holding in
past agonies, have learned
to build their own happiness
little by little.

You'll know them: a certain kind
of tiredness around
eyes that are smiling;
the way they laugh, the whole
of life in their laughter, all
its terrifying brightness
on the border with death.

No one can laugh like them.
They know they've lived on.

And now listen to me well
hear what I say:
they are the only people
who know the path to Paradise.

Translated by Ruth Valentine and Erif Reson

Eduardo Embry Morales

Eduardo Embry Morales was born in Valparaiso, Chile, in 1932. In the 1960s he won many prizes for his poetry in Chile. During the Popular Unity government of President Salvador Allende, he produced and presented radio programmes. He left his country after being held in the prison ship *El Lebu* at the time of the 1973 military coup. He came to Scotland with the help of the British Council and the University of Glasgow. He is a lecturer in Spanish language and Latin American poetry and has published several books of his own poetry and of his research into Latin American poetry of the seventeenth to nineteenth centuries. He is an Honorary Fellow at the University of Southampton and a Research Fellow at the Hartley Institute there. In 1998, a collection of his poems, *Breviareo de la Memoria*, was published by the University of Valparaiso.

Every Day I Make Ready

Every day I make ready
for the day that you leave me
or for the day that I die
or for the day that,
at a crossroads,
I take the wrong turning and can't find you
or I take the right turning
and you are the one who doesn't turn up,
or perhaps, who knows,
we'll grow old together.
Even so
every day I make ready
for the day that we part for ever.

Translated by Penelope Turpin

Tin Moe

Tin Moe was born in Burma in 1933 and his original name was U Ba Gyan. After 1988 he became a member of the National League for Democracy and published a number of poems about the democracy movement. In 1991 he was appointed editor-in-chief of the literary magazine *Pe-Hpu-Hlwa*, but was arrested after only one issue and the magazine was closed. After being held without charge for six months, he is thought to have been sentenced to four years in June 1992. 'The Years We Didn't See the Dawn' was written shortly after the military assumption of power in September 1988.

The Years We Didn't See the Dawn

Half asleep, half awake, a time of
dreaming dreams
I wanted to walk but did not know which road to take
Half unknowing, my days are running out
My paunch thickens and my neck folds sag as I grow older,
A time of getting nowhere, I have passed through all this
    time
Unheeding, as in a train one passes stations by.

As a young man, I met with Lenin
But growing older, I would like to meet Lincoln . . .

The way we live now, submitting reports loaded with lies,
Recording 'yes, sir, certainly, sir' onto tapes filled with
misinformation,
Our smart 'party' jackets now all creased and musty.
We are treated like tea-flasks, put here, sent there at our
bosses' bidding,
Robots, our lives without joy, we merely nod our heads.
At this time, we are not poetry, we are not human,
This is not life, this is just so much wastepaper . . .

We have bartered away our lives for falsehood
And now we have reached old age, at death's very door,
surely these times should be put on record as
'The years we didn't see the dawn'?

Sharnush Parsipur

Sharnush Parsipur (born 1946) is from Iran. She is a novelist and short-story writer and most of her work, including *The Dog and the Long Winter*, has been banned in Iran for the last ten years. She was arrested in 1981 and remained in prison until 1986. She was rearrested and briefly detained on two further occasions in 1990 and 1991. She now lives in the USA.

The Executions

Bored as I was, I began, along with a few other inmates, to make worry beads. The dough of the bread was the material we used to form the beads, and we used powdered paint to color them.

At this time, prisoners were being regularly taken for interrogation. They usually wore oversized slippers to these ordeals. The reason for this was that they were regularly whipped on their feet, and in consequence the feet would swell. Had they not taken their oversized slippers, they would have had to walk back to the cell on bare bruised feet.

The daily departure of these prisoners to the prosecutor's office created an incredible atmosphere of terror in the cell. I continued to make worry beads and observe my cellmates. The number of prisoners had drastically increased.

The number of prisoners beaten was also on the rise. I remember well Shahin, a dark-faced girl. She belonged to one of the leftist groups. I asked her to show me her bruises. She laughed and said that because of her dark skin, the bruises could not be seen. I followed each case with avid curiosity. It seemed in some cases that the whole body was one big bruise.

The next night I saw Shahin in the bathroom again. She seemed happy as she chatted to her friend – apparently she had gone to another interrogation, and now felt that the danger had passed. A couple of days later, she seemed rather nervous again: and that night she was summoned once more to the prosecutor's office. The next day, her name appeared on the list of those who had been executed. I had by then become a friend of her friend and I asked her about Shahin. Apparently, Shahin's crime was to have been the driver of a car in the trunk of which a small printing press had been hidden. On the last day of her life, Shahin had told her friend that she thought she was going to be executed. She knew this because the interrogator had fondled her breasts, and that was a sure sign of doom.

The truth is I have never seen a political prisoner who had been sexually abused or molested. There was a rumor that virgins condemned to die were married to the Revolutionary Guards before their execution. According to tradition, if a virgin girl is buried, she will take a man with her. Since no one who was executed ever came back to speak of their experience, I was never able to verify this rumor. Shahin's words are my only proof. I also know of a couple of prisoners who came very close to have sexual relations with their interrogators. In one case the cause was the girl's clever attempt to avoid torture. The second case was a heated love affair between a prisoner and her interrogator.

Toward the end of September, the number of prisoners who could not walk was on the increase. They had been badly whipped on the soles of their feet. After a while a swollen lump, the size of an orange, would appear on the bottom of their feet. One of the biggest problems for these prisoners was walking to the bathroom. Some found a clever solution: they turned a big metal container of cheese into a chamber pot. They installed a thin layer of foam around the rim of the pot; three people would embrace the wounded prisoner and gingerly lower her on to it.

One night, as we all lay in the dark, I decided to go to the bathroom, hoping to avoid the long line in the morning. It was one o'clock in the morning. Prisoners were lined up next to each other on the floor. They were all awake. There was absolute silence in the cell. Something ominous was in the atmosphere. There was no line for the toilet. Instead, a few prisoners stood around and took turns to climb up on the water-heater and look out. When I approached, I saw one of the girls trembling. Although we were not friends, she held my arm and quietly said that the bodies of prisoners were being lined up in the yard. From about eleven o'clock that night, a piercing sound had been heard at more or less regular intervals. One of the prisoners suggested that the authorities were constructing a new visiting center and what we heard was the sound of steel being unloaded. The girl I was with became visibly more shaken when the sound was heard again. I asked *her* about the sound. She said it was machine-gun fire.

By the time that long and bitter night finally passed we had counted more than two hundred and fifty 'coups de grâce'. In the newspapers the next day, I found the names of more than three hundred people who had been executed.

The following day was even more awful for everyone in the block. They took a few prisoners from each block to the office of the prosecutor. There, after summary trials lasting between two and five minutes, the prisoners were divided into two lines. One line was taken to be executed; the other was returned to the cells. The intent was probably to bring terror to everyone. Many of the prisoners who were called to trial that night behaved abnormally for many months afterwards. I saw one of them occasionally fall as she walked, and then get up and continue as though nothing had happened. Another sat the whole night gazing at the toothbrushes, the towels, and the jackets of the executed prisoners . . .

That same day, they brought Holou to our block. She was a shy girl and stood in a corner motionless. I asked her her name. 'Holou,' she replied. It was a habit of the Mujahadin to give a false name at the time of arrest. In prison, they would call one another by names of flowers, fruits and animals. The leftists also had the same habit. Holou, Persian for peach, truly resembled her name.

I told Holou that I would like to know her real name.

With tears in her eyes, she said she had already died four times. She explained how from the moment of her arrest, up until our conversation, the guards had simulated her execution four times. Twice the Revolutionary Guards had stormed a bus ferrying prisoners, pretending to go on a rampage. On another occasion, they had stood her against a wall, told her she was going to be shot, and then fired blanks at her. I forget the details of the fourth experience. As we talked, it was clear that something *had* truly died in her: she was only fifteen years old and I was filled with silent rage about her torments.

Another of the prisoners, named Golshan, seemed deeply melancholic. I was told that only last week her father, along with other monarchists, had been executed. I tried to help this young girl and soon became friends with her. Before her incarceration, she had performed her prayers religiously, but had quit them upon her arrest. She had been at an engineering college somewhere in England; around Easter time she had returned to Iran to marry her fiancé. Her father was a member of a monarchist group and as bad luck would have it, when Revolutionary Guards raided her father's office to arrest him and other members of the group, she was in the office. As she claimed, and I have no reason to doubt it, her only participation in the group was typing one of their letters. She was arrested along with everybody else. During interrogation she had behaved badly, being utterly intransigent on matters of rather dubious significance. For instance, she had refused to wear a veil or to remove her nail polish from her fingers. The sight of her father's execution changed her radically. I think she tried to compensate for her father's timorous behavior during his trial by her own valor.

While in Evin prison, she had a dream that she related to me. She dreamed that she was engulfed inside an octopus. A big tendril forcefully entered the entrails and plucked someone from inside each organ, placing them in another tendril. Golshan began to scream, 'Take me too! Take me too!' and she ran after the big tendril. The tendril deposited the abducted people on top of a hill and Golshan heard the voice of the Octopus saying, 'I just had this hankering to bring them out here.'

The dream was important. In prison, the killing grounds were called 'hills'. In hindsight, I regret I did not try at the time to analyse her dream for her. I only told her, 'Golshan, be careful.' As was her habit, she took some pills and hid under a blanket. Under the blanket was her only place of solace.

Toward the end of November, overcrowding in the prison reached an explosive point. There were more than three hundred and fifty people crammed in our few cells. Every night, a group of prisoners were forced to stand in a corner, because there was not enough room for everyone to sit down. Summary trials and mass executions had become routine . . . I was tired and disheartened. I felt the weight of all the corpses on my shoulders. In one way, though, I felt happy to be in prison in these treacherous times; I knew that if I were free, and did not take any steps to protest the executions, I would have for ever hated myself. But the unfolding catastrophe was much bigger than anything I could do, bigger even than anything a political group could do. In captivity, one is not tormented with these problems, for there is *definitely* nothing one can do. I knew that when the sad history of these days came to be written down, then at least my role would be clear.

Albert Camus, in his interpretation of the Sisyphus myth – the man who had killed his son and was commanded by the gods to spend eternity pushing a rock up a steep hill so that it can roll down again – claims that the man was happy because he need make no choices. Now, in prison, in times of bloody and banal brutality, I too was happy because I need not make any choices. I had not asked to be in this position, but I made no efforts to escape from it, leaving my fate in the hands of the Hezbollah.

Translated by Abbas Milani

Ken Saro-Wiwa

Ken Saro-Wiwa (1941–1995) was one of Nigeria's best-known writers. He was a member of the Ogoni tribe, whose land has been exploited by multinational companies extracting oil. Ken Saro-Wiwa opposed this action and the military governments in power in Nigeria. He was arrested and charged with incitement to murder, and was executed by hanging on 10 November 1995.

The True Prison

It is not the leaking roof
Nor the singing mosquitoes
In the damp, wretched cell
It is not the clank of the key
As the warden locks you in
It is not the measly rations
Unfit for beast or man
Nor yet the emptiness of day
Dipping into the blankness of night
It is not
It is not
It is not

It is the lies that have been drummed
Into your ears for a generation
It is the security agent running amok
Executing callous calamitous orders
In exchange for a wretched meal a day
The magistrate writing into her book
A punishment she knows is undeserved
The moral decrepitude
The mental ineptitude
The meat of dictators
Cowardice masking as obedience
Lurking in our denigrated souls
It is fear damping trousers

That we dare not wash
It is this
It is this
It is this
Dear friend, turns our free world
Into a dreary prison

Fatma

Fatma, an Alevi Kurd, was born in a remote village in central Turkey in 1960. She was tortured because of her membership of the TKP-ML (Communist Party of Turkey – Marxist-Leninist). Alevis are Muslims whose beliefs and rituals vary from region to region. Retaining strong elements of pre-Islamic Turkish and Iranian religions, they are more closely related to the Shia branch of Islam than the mainstream Sunni orthodoxy most Turks follow. As a result, they have traditionally endured much hostility. Often fiercely secular, the Alevis are seen as natural allies by Turkey's radical left, and as natural targets by right-wing extremists and Islamic fundamentalists.

Recent examples of their persecution include a mob attack on an Alevi cultural festival in a hotel in the city of Sivas in 1993, when police stood idly by while thirty-seven people burned to death. That was followed in 1995 by gun attacks on five teahouses in an Alevi neighbourhood in Istanbul. Police later fired indiscriminately on protesters, killing fifteen. Fatma lost a cousin in the Sivas fire.

Testimony

We grew up hating the government. When we were kids we would cry and ask why we couldn't go to school. There was just a little room in the house of a neighbour where my uncle taught us. There would be twenty girls in there, all ages, five to eighteen. Later they did send us a teacher, but he was a Sunni Muslim. His wife would say in front of his students, 'Come and wash your hands. You have been dealing with Alevis.'

We didn't have any problem with the Sunni villages nearby. We didn't talk much with them, or marry, but we didn't fight. The government pushed people to fight each other, to make itself strong.

In winter there was a lot of snow. It would come up to the windows. Roads would be blocked and a lot of pregnant women died but the government didn't care. They just came to our village for taxes. To them we were two problems. We were Kurds, and we were Alevis. We weren't even allowed to speak our own language.

When I was young, people were frightened of the government. Soldiers would come sometimes and ask if there were any terrorists about. Once when I was about twelve they came and said, 'We have heard you have guns.' They were in the village chief's house – my father and uncle were there. They hit them and put guns to the chief's head.

They came back time and time again until in the end the village bought guns to give them and they put them on TV saying they had been seized from our village. In court one man said, 'I've sold a cow to buy a gun and if you threaten me again I will sell the other cow and get you another gun.'

When I was about sixteen my daddy rented a house in the city so the little ones could go to school. I was the oldest of two boys and four girls. My job was to look after them while my parents stayed in the village. I loved school myself and would cry but my daddy said I had to help him this way.

Later one of my brothers got a job with the local council but when they realized he was Alevi they pushed him out. They sacked about fifteen Alevis, who went on hunger strike in front of the council building. My brother was with them. After three days the police came and took him to prison. I didn't want my dad to know but two months later he came to the city and found out.

When my dad went to try to find him, the police told him they didn't know where my brother was – they were looking for him themselves. But a few days later he reappeared. He was very bad – bruised all over.

We took him to a doctor, an Alevi, but he said he couldn't give us any proof of torture. It would be the end of his career. After the hunger strike, the movement knew we were on their side, and a little later I was asked to help a Kurdish couple and their child who were in hiding.

I was scared but I took the risk for the little boy – at first he couldn't walk. I was told they had been employed by the council too but when I saw the boy's feet I thought maybe they had come from the mountains.

A little later one of their friends was arrested and revealed under torture where they were staying. Fortunately, we were warned that neighbours had been seen pointing out our house to people who looked like policemen and we were able to get them away. My brother was arrested but they had to let him go because they couldn't find any proof.

My little sister started school soon afterwards and she was talking above herself, saying, 'We are Alevis. We are against the government.' After that, they came and arrested me.

They gave me a ten-page statement to sign. First of all they gave me blank paper and said, 'Write it all down. We know the couple stayed with you.' They even knew the colour of a dress I had been wearing at a wedding I had been to but when they said they knew I had met the couple outside such and such a building and it was the wrong building, I realized that they didn't know everything and that made me strong.

They said they knew someone was using me. I thought I had better write something so I started to make a statement about my life story and they became very angry. They laid me on the floor and stood on my fingers. I thought that the moment they touched me I would do anything for them but instead I became very strong. I was surprised. Then I was kicked with boots and blacked out.

In the cell people had written on the wall 'Don't be scared' and that made me strong too, although there was blood there as well, some of it old and some of it new. They kept me for fifteen days altogether – blindfolded a lot of the time.

Sometimes they touched me sexually, in a disgusting way, and once they stripped me naked in front of my brother. 'Don't worry,' he said. 'I have to watch but I can't see anything.'

On another occasion they placed a Kurdish man either side of me, prisoners who were wet and shaking. While the officers took a photograph, I asked, 'Did they hurt you?' and the policeman said, 'Shut up.' One boy patted my arm and said, 'Don't worry. We are OK.' It was as though he was my brother.

The worst time, though, was when the police took me to hear a Kurdish girl being tortured in another room. She was screaming, screaming for her parents.

When I was released I remained politically active and was arrested another five times until eventually I had to flee. My father sold a tractor to pay off the police and I came to Britain. That was ten years ago.

Sometimes now I can't remember the faces of my family and that makes me cry, but there was no way I could avoid doing what I did. Two of my younger sisters have also been tortured for belonging to a left-wing group. The repression still goes on. It affects every aspect of our lives.

BYSTANDERS

People watch torture happening, others know about it and do nothing. Personal and public morality shifts. The sense of right and wrong is altered.

Babek

It is too easy to judge people for not speaking out about the atrocities they knew to be happening. When a country is surrounded by the shadow of terror, how can you expect people to sacrifice themselves? Once I had come out of prison, if they had given me shelter, their house would have been burned down. The only people in my country who were bystanders were the ones who were supporting the regime.

But the thing is that people did put themselves at risk. My neighbours helped my brother and me when they hid us. And when my friend died under torture, his body ironed by hot metal and broken, the government wouldn't let people go and see his ageing father. But my father and I went and sat with him in his lonely house and soon others followed. People were arrested but still more came to sit with him.

Sometimes you are forced to be a bystander. To be unable to do anything, say anything, is the worst kind of torture; to be made crazy by sights you've seen. Once they tied four men, four freedom fighters, to a stone and shot them from their legs upwards, slowly wishing them to suffer in agony even for the last few minutes of their poor lives. I had to watch it happen. Their blood flooded down into the river and the river flowed into the sea, carrying the message, the final outcome of that torture.

As I am writing this, I know someone behind a locked door is screaming under torture. As you are reading this, a child is being beaten. But the voice of politics is louder, much louder, and easily covers the scream of those being tortured. The real bystander is the one who is in a position to speak freely but does not.

Erich Fried

Erich Fried (1921–1988) was born in Vienna. He fled Austria in 1938 after his father had been killed by the Gestapo; he came to live in London, where he tried to help others escape. After World War II, he worked in the German service of the BBC. His work became popular in Germany in the 1960s and he often travelled there to give readings. His political and love poems became best sellers. He translated the works of Shakespeare, Dylan Thomas and Sylvia Plath.

What Happens

It has happened
and it goes on happening
and will happen again
if nothing happens to stop it

The innocent know nothing
because they are too innocent
and the guilty know nothing
because they are too guilty

The poor do not notice
because they are too poor
and the rich do not notice
because they are too rich

The stupid shrug their shoulders
because they are too stupid
and the clever shrug their shoulders
because they are too clever

The young do not care
because they are too young
and the old do not care
because they are too old

That is why nothing happens
to stop it
and that is why it has happened
and goes on happening and will happen again

Translated by Stuart Hood

Nina Cassian

Nina Cassian was born in Romania in 1924. She was a leading figure in Romania for over forty years when, in 1985, during a visit to New York, her satires of the Ceaușescu regime were discovered copied into a friend's diary. The friend was tortured to death and Cassian's house was ransacked by the authorities and her publications were banned. She is also a composer and translator. She has lived in New York since 1985.

Horizon

And yet there must exist
a zone of salvation.
Sad are the countries
who don't have outlets to water,
dull are the people who have no outlet from themselves
toward another outlet, even greater.

Translated by Andrea Deletant and Brenda Walker

Jack Mapanje

Jack Mapanje was born in 1944 in Kadango village, Malawi. He became a teacher of linguistics. His first book, *Of Chameleons and Gods*, was published in 1981. On its second reprint it was banned by the government of Malawi and Mapanje was put in Mikuyu Prison for over three years, although no charges were ever brought against him. He was released in May 1991 after prolonged protests from writers and activists round the world. This extract is from his second book of poems, *The Chattering Wagtails of Mikuyu Prison*.

Fears from Mikuyu Cells for Our Loves

Our neighbours' nerves behind those
Trimmed pine hedges of Chingwe's Hole
And the strategies they'll adopt when

They are approached by the Special
Branch, are familiar but horrify;
We rehearsed their betrayals weekly:

'Where did you first meet, I mean,
What did he often boast about in bars;
When he played darts, what jokes?

Didn't he, in your considered view,
Behave in a manner prejudicial? So,
He bent even those straight lectures!

Did your children ever mix with his
And how often did your wife share
Home-ground maize flour with his?'

We recycled other fears ad nauseam too
And what tricks to perform to thrive;
Only the victim's hour did we not know.

I recall, when our neighbour was
Taken eleven years ago, secret tears
On my wife's cheeks because visiting

His wife and kids or offering them
Our sweet potatoes in broad day was
A crime, her husband had just been

Invented 'rebel'; on the third day
University Office quickly issued her
Exit visa to her husband's village.

The feasts of our singular friends
We also reran: 'His detention was
Overdue, those poems! Don't mention

That name in my office; I hear he
Refused to apologize, how typical!
How is that woman and her kids still

Occupying that University house?
Those conferences that he loved, it's us
Going now. Has he reached Mikuyu then?

We thought it was another joke!'
Today, I see your delicate laughter
And what abuse they'll hurl at you

Dear children, dear mother, my dear
Wife as your 'rebel' dad confronts
The wagtail shit of Mikuyu Prison:

'Shore up their brittle feet, Lord!'

Dennis Brutus

Dennis Brutus was born in 1924 in Harare, Zimbabwe, but grew up in South Africa. He taught English and Afrikaans in high school for fourteen years until he was dismissed in 1962 for his anti-apartheid activities. While studying law at the University of Witwatersrand, Johannesburg, he became involved in the struggle against racism in South African sports. Later he was arrested, banned, shot in an attempt to leave South Africa and sentenced to eighteen months' hard labour. In 1966 he left the country and has spent much of the rest of his life teaching in the USA, where he was granted asylum in 1983. He remains committed to the defence of human rights. He is one of South Africa's best-known and most highly regarded poets.

Their Behaviour

Their guilt
is not so very different from ours:
– who has not joyed in the arbitrary exercise of
    power
or grasped for himself what might have been
    another's
and who has not used superior force in the
    moment when he could,
(and who of us has not been tempted to these
    things?) –
so, in their guilt,
the bared ferocity of teeth,
chest-thumping challenge and defiance,
the deafening clamour of their prayers
to a deity made in the image of their prejudice
which drowns the voice of conscience,
is mirrored our predicament
but on a social, massive, organized scale
which magnifies enormously
as the private deshabille of love
becomes obscene in orgies.

(Blood River Day 1965)

88

Sheila Cassidy

Dr Sheila Cassidy was born in the UK and educated there and in Australia. She qualified in medicine in 1963 at Oxford University and then embarked initially on a career in plastic surgery. In December 1971 she went to Chile in order to gain further surgical experience and in 1975 was detained and tortured for treating a wounded revolutionary and spent two months in prison. She was expelled from Chile in December 1975. After her return she was very active in human-rights work, lecturing widely at home and abroad. In 1978 she entered a convent but left after eighteen months, returning to the full-time practice of medicine in July 1980, working as Senior House Officer in the Radiotherapy Department in Plymouth.

She was Medical Director of St Luke's Hospice in Plymouth 1982–93, and palliative care specialist at Plymouth General Hospital 1993–96; she was then appointed psycho-oncologist, caring for the emotional needs of cancer patients. She will complete her training as a psychotherapist in 1999. She remains heavily involved in education in psychological care for cancer patients, lecturing widely in Plymouth, other areas in the UK and also abroad.

The Bystanders

All I could see was his shoes: immaculate suede desert boots, and the bottom of his trousers: beige cavalry twill, to match the boots. Even with my blindfold fairly loose, I had no possibility of seeing his face, and after hearing his voice, I didn't really want to. It was an educated voice, as you might expect in a professional person, but it had a chilling quality I had never before heard in a doctor, a mixture of dislike and scorn that filled me anew with fear and anger. On the day after my interrogation and torture, I had been taken to 'see' or rather to be seen by the doctor. Naive as ever, I assumed that he would accord me the courtesy which I was accustomed to receiving at the hands of my medical colleagues. I could not, however, have been more mistaken. When I told him that I had vaginal bleeding following the insertion, during interrogation, of an electrode, he replied coolly, 'Periods are normal in women, doctor.'

It's difficult to convey how angry this remark made me, for it was as if he himself had struck me in the face to humiliate me. What really hurt was the realization that he didn't give a damn for me as I stood there, dishevelled and afraid, my jeans filthy and caked with a mixture of my own blood and that of Enriquetta, the Columbian Fathers' housekeeper who had been shot dead when I was arrested.

It's over twenty years now since I was arrested and tortured for treating a wounded revolutionary, but the memories of the pain of torture, the terror and utter desolation of three weeks in solitary confinement, are still with me. True, the impact has been mitigated by years of psychotherapy and by a return visit to Santiago, but the scars remain. It is the same, I believe, for all of us, the men and women who have been detained, stripped naked, hurt and humiliated. We are all left with a thin veneer over our pain and the outraged question: how could one human being do this to another, and how could others stand by and watch it happen? What are we doing, when we in this country turn away from other people's suffering? What is it that happens in the human heart to block the natural flow of compassion that is an intrinsic part of our make-up?

This problem of our individual responsibility for the pain of others is one that has plagued me for many years. In the first flush of my enthusiasm for human rights work I would delight in making my audiences feel uncomfortable. 'The poor are as near as the nearest bank!' I would proclaim, and in some ways I was right. But of course, it isn't quite as simple as that, as I have learned to my cost. We in the developed world have our own stresses and difficulties, our own individual poverty. True, it is not usually a question of not having enough to eat, but our lives are complicated and the needs of any one individual difficult to assess.

Most ordinary people love little children, are gentle with the old and the sick and are frequently capable of heroic behaviour to help a fellow in distress. And yet many ordinary people are also capable of hardening their hearts, of ignoring the suffering of others. I do it, most of us do it, every day. Is it compassion fatigue that ails me when I throw a handful of charitable requests into the bin, or when I sit with glazed eyes watching yet another television portrayal of hungry children or tortured refugees? Perhaps T. S. Eliot understood it when he wrote 'humankind cannot bear too much reality'.

SURVIVAL

People find strength and courage in many different ways, without losing their humanity.

Babek

I determined to survive because I had to tell my story, I had to be a witness. It was a mission because I believed that this regime could not survive; there is no ultimate escape for the power of darkness. Light will appear, a spark will interrupt that evilness. I planned nice things and told stories. I thought that when I got out I would be wiser and tougher.

When being interrogated I determined not to aggravate my captors, I thought I would keep my dignity but not be too rude, not talk too much and never sign anything. I would say 'yes' rather than 'no'. If they asked for names, I would give them some, but only those I knew to be safe, such as people they already knew about.

Only one time I broke down and lost my temper. A friend who had been visiting me disappeared. The authorities had caught him taking messages out; they broke him and killed him. On New Year's Day in my country we give presents; they gave his parents a sack with his bloodied clothes.

For some of the time I was in a cell on my own. There were bloodstains on the wall. I felt the presence of other prisoners, ones who had been there before me. I wanted to be able to tell the stories of the bloodstains if I got out.

There was an old uneducated man who was Kurdish. He was illiterate and so anything they put in front of him he would 'sign' with his thumb. I said to him, 'You teach me Kurdish and I will teach you to read and write', and that is what I did. I saw him write his first letter. I felt stronger and that I had some power even in this place because of my experience with this Kurdish man. I can forget about the lashes and I came out alive. He is now part of my survival.

Alex Polari

Alex Polari (born 1950) was active in the student movement in Brazil in the late 1960s and later joined an armed opposition group. He was arrested in May 1971 at the age of twenty-one; he was tortured and sentenced by a military court to eighteen years' imprisonment.

The Early Days of Torture

It was no easy thing those days
to go hooded across
the distance from cell
to torture chamber
and there come out with roars
more hideous than I ever heard before

There were days when the pirouettes on the parrot's perch*
seemed ridiculous and shaming
and we were still capable of blushing
at the sadistic jokes of our executioners

There were days in which all prospects
were on the far side of blackness
and all expectations
came down to the rather sceptical hope
of not getting beaten or having electric shocks

There were other moments
when the hours wasted away
in waiting for the bolt on the door which led
to the hands of the specialists
in our agony

There were also times
when the only possible worry
was about having some toilet paper
or something to eat and a fork to eat it with

knowing the name of the warder on duty
holding on to the hope of a first visit
which was like a guarantee of life
an official stamp of survival
and the status of political prisoner

Afterwards the situation got better
and it was even possible to suffer
to feel distraught, to read
to love, to be jealous
and all the other pleasant stupidities
that on the outside we take
for crucial experiences.

Translated by Alicia and Nick Caistor

---

* The 'parrot's perch' is a form of torture: a horizontal bar stands about five feet from the floor and from this the prisoner is suspended. His wrists are tied to his legs, the bar is passed between the legs and hands and then hoisted.

Eric Lomax

Eric Lomax (born 1919) grew up in Scotland in the 1930s, a devoted railway enthusiast.

In 1941, he was sent to Malaya as a member of the Royal Corps of Signals. Taken prisoner after the fall of Singapore, he was put to work on the infamous Burma–Siam railway, which cost the lives of 250,000 men. He helped to build an illicit radio, so that the prisoners could follow the news of the war.

The discovery of the radio by the Japanese resulted in two years of dreadful torture, starvation and distress. Among his tormentors was a young English-speaking Japanese man attached to the secret police. Eric never forgot his voice or his face. He spent half a century after the war alone with his experiences; he felt that there was no one with whom he could share them.

In 1987, Eric came to the Medical Foundation; he describes his first meeting as 'walking through a door into an unexplored world, a world of caring and special understanding'.

By coincidence, he then discovered that his Japanese interrogator was alive; he found out where he was and travelled to meet him.

His life was saved from bitterness and the need for revenge by an extraordinary will to remember and forgive.

Extract from *The Railway Man*

The radio was primitive, little more than a crystal set, tuned to a single frequency and incapable of sending a signal; it was also a simple masterpiece. It was about 9 inches long by 4 inches wide, and fitted snugly into a coffee tin with a false top, which we filled with ground nuts. It sat there innocently by Thew's bed, a rusty silver tin can hiding the valves and condensers.

The routine was the same each evening. Prisoners would be detailed to stand around the camp and warn us about the approach of any Japanese, many of them not even being told why they were doing it. Thew would couple the set to the aerial, which was hidden in the rafters, switch on the apparatus and burrow down under his blanket with the headphones on. He was always the operator, since he was by far the best person to deal with any tuning problems if the signals were lost or distorted. The news bulletin took about ten minutes, and he would note down the main items with his pencil as he listened. The precious scrap of paper was handed around a small group afterwards, as Thew dismantled the set and placed it back in its hiding place. I still remember his strong, careful handling of the crude little machine, the tenderness of the true craftsman.

We were stealing back information from our captors. We heard about the victories of the Solomon Islands, of New Guinea and Guadalcanal, and that the Germans had been stopped in Russia and driven back in North Africa. From November 1942, when our radio started operating, we felt again that we might eventually be liberated, that we were on the winning side.

Lance Thew could be a hair-raising innocent. We were free to ramble around the area, and often came upon small Siamese settlements. Thew had stumbled on an 'empty Buddhist temple', as he put it wonderingly, with a small gold-leaf-covered statue of Buddha in a dusty niche, and a few dead flowers around the image. He helped himself to the statue: a nice souvenir of Siam. When we discovered it in his bed-space, we ordered him vehemently to return it. We were afraid of some frightening chain of repercussions; less rationally, we dreaded the fixed smile of the deity and the feeling of bad karma that grew around him. I wondered later, and not idly, whether what happened was a kind of punishment for this blasphemy.

Perhaps what Thew did was just another symptom of our devil-may-care attitude, our defiance of the Japanese and of imprisonment. We still felt invincible. Surrender hadn't brought weakness and submission.

María Eugenia Bravo Calderara

María Eugenia Bravo Calderara was born in Santiago, Chile, in 1940. At the time of the coup in 1973, she was a lecturer at the Universidad de Chile. She was taken to the National Stadium, tortured and imprisoned, but finally escaped to England in 1975. She has lived there ever since. Her first poems were kept by her mother, who buried them in her garden until later they were sent to Switzerland in a diplomatic bag. María Bravo was not able to visit her mother until 1990.

She has published her own volume of poetry and her work has appeared in magazines and anthologies. Love and exile and the memory of prison have been at the core of her poetry. As a literary critic, she is also the author of a book on Pablo Neruda's poetry.

Private Soldier

For you, short, dark, under-fed, with sweaty hands,
who know nothing of grammar, accents and declensions,
your turn had come that year
to be called up for military service,
in the army at the lowest rank,
just a private with no stripes.
Today I sing to you.

Because
when I had no eyes you lent me yours
and when I was cold you lent me your coat.

Because
at that time when fear and isolation
were at their most overwhelming,
you rolled me a cigarette.
You brought me a painkiller, ointment,
delivered an urgent note to my family.

How we cared for each other in those dumb hours,
your shivering was my shivering
and one and the same demon dominated our lives.
I know about your powerlessness
in the vicious night
and your despair under the shrunken sun.

I did not see you and I saw you.
I never knew your name
or where you came from,
the roll-up, the painkiller, the blind eye turned,
the anonymous biscuit, the delivered note.
You did not tell me your name or where your home was
but I know what you are called. Human.

Translated by Dinah Livingstone

Ala Mehrzad

Dr Ala Mehrzad is an Iranian refugee who was imprisoned for five years for his political beliefs and activities. He now lives in Britain and is rebuilding his life as a doctor.

Dr Mehrzad worked with Sonja Linden (Writer-in-Residence of the Medical Foundation) to write this piece.

A Short Journey with the Moon on a Dark Night

It was during my first days in the general section of the prison, where I had been moved after being in solitary confinement for several months. I found myself in a crowded cell with ninety other political prisoners – 'Number 7 Down' it was known as – a large room with two windows, located in the basement. We were in the part of the prison called Section Two, which consisted of a two-storey building with six cells on the ground floor and seven in the basement. There was a yard, which, for the first months of my arrival, we were not allowed to use. Section Two was situated in a valley and surrounded by high walls, behind which we could see the distant hills.

Our cell was so crowded that everybody had to sleep on their sides, there wasn't enough room for people to lie on their backs or stomachs. This plus the fact that there was no free access to toilets and sinks just added to the physical and psychological pressure in the prison.

Among the prisoners there was a young man with a very good singing voice, who used to sing popular and revolutionary songs. He was a second-year chemistry student and we soon grew very close, even though our political views were very different. Together we would stand by one of the windows at night, talking about our feelings, worries and desires. At night the pressure of sadness and loneliness even in the midst of a crowded cell would increase. The pressure would begin at sunset each afternoon and gradually rise until it reached its peak when darkness fell on the outside world like a heavy veil of grief and mourning. It was a time when our fears and sense of aloneness were intensified, but little by little we tried to overcome these feelings by trying to imagine what might be happening on the other side of the high, triple prison walls during those long dark nights.

And so we discovered that night and darkness had some constructive, positive aspects to them. Night was frequently a time, after all, when children came into the world. It was also a time when courageous men and women would emerge to write slogans. The darkness of night gave protection to brave people in hiding. And so it was part of life. Standing by the window at night we managed to achieve some sort of imaginative interaction with the outside world. Someone out there was writing a love letter. A couple were kissing. A young man was running down an alley in order not to be arrested by the militia. These were some of the scenes we imagined. And in addition we would softly sing:

> One moonshining night
> The moon would come to my dreams
> She would take me outside the prison
> To the city
> To the crossroads
> To the streets
> To the alleys
> I would call out loudly
> Where are you, martyrs of this city?
> Are you awake or sleeping?
> Can you hear me?
> The moon would take me to the garden
> The garden of vines and
> A solitary old willow
> Happy and full of hope
> Great hope and the desire for freedom
> We would walk towards a spring of fresh water

> Where a beautiful angel might come
> And dip her feet into the water.
> She would comb her long hair
> She might take my hand
> She could take me away from the prison.   •

Thus our night journeys with the moon continued. We talked about them with our friends who responded in a number of ways. Some of them disapproved of our 'night flights', dismissing them as too romantic or poetic and thus a potential threat to our ability to cope with the pressures of life in prison, with the cruelty of the prison officers. They felt we should be concentrating our energies on the reality of life in prison instead of engaging in imaginative pursuits. A smaller group of friends, however, clearly could identify with what we were doing and even began to do likewise. As usual the majority of the prisoners had no strong opinions either way, they were part of what I came to recognise as the passive section of the prison population.

I should make it clear at this point that these night journeys were not just poetic experiences, they were, in fact, important psychological aids to survival, especially at that particular time when the pressures on political prisoners was especially intense. None of us were trained professional politicians or revolutionary leaders, and so we had to start from scratch in finding strategies for emotional survival, if we did not want to break down. We were aware of the dangers of thinking about the outside world, of its potentially weakening effect as far as our determination to resist was concerned. Finding the right balance was sometimes a difficult task. There were very real problems that we had to face daily individually and collectively, such as interrogation, torture, hunger and overcrowding.

Oktay Rifat

Oktay Rifat (1914–1988) was born in Turkey, the son of a poet. He completed his studies in Paris and returned to Turkey to work for several years as a legal adviser to the State Railways administration. In 1941, he was one of three poets who came together to write a revolutionary collection of Turkish poems titled *Garip (Strange)* in which the language, stories and lives of ordinary people are revealed with understanding, humour and deep feeling. He said later in an interview that 'the job of poetry is to find a remedy for social ills'.

The Embrace

Warm me this night,
O my trust in freedom
wrap me warm
against my mattress thin and blankets torn.
Out there is unimaginable cold and wind,
outside – oppression
torture
out there – death.
O my trust in freedom
enter deep,
warm me through this night.
On my palm a place is ready
for my hands,
on my thighs a place
to lean your knees.
Enclose me,
sheathe me,
wrap me warm,
O my trust in freedom
wrap me warm this night.

Translated by Ruth Christie

Bao Ruowang

Bao Ruowang was born in Beijing. His father was Corsican and his mother was Chinese. He was arrested in 1957 and spent seven years in prison and labour camps. When he was released, he wrote *Prisoner of Mao* (with Rudolph Chelminski), from which this extract is taken. Bao Ruowang later moved to Paris.

Three Scenes from a Labour Camp

Food Substitute

By the end of November I had picked up the rhythm of existence at Qinghe.[1] I was a professional prisoner by then, and felt that I knew how to survive any of the physical or spiritual trials the place could throw at me. In the end I did survive, but it was a much closer thing than I thought it would be. If I was able to adapt to the harshness of the climate, the rough working conditions, the intellectual humiliation and even the semi-starvation of drastically reduced rations, there was little I or any of the others could do about the recurrent waves of disease and debilitation which chose to visit us. As Solzhenitsyn wrote of the Soviet camps, many better men than I broke and many stronger ones died. The strange laws of chance always play.

In the thirteen months that remained before me at that prison farm I was plunged into such a series of personal experiences and human encounters that the outside world I rejoined afterward often seems pale and less significant by comparison. My head so swims with images of what I went through myself, or what others told me about, or what I learned of by accident, that if they come out here in a somewhat kaleidoscopic jumble, forgive me: they are the essence of what it is like to be down and out in a Chinese labour camp.

The signal that truly desperate times were upon us came in early December, when a horse-drawn cart entered the compound and a prisoner detail began unloading the cargo: dark brown sheets of an unknown material, rigid and light, each one measuring about three by five feet. No one had any idea of what they were. Two weeks later we were called into the auditorium to hear the answer. The stuff was paper pulp, and we were going to eat it. Food Substitute, the prison officials called it – *daishipin*. I'll never forget the words. Since there wasn't enough food to go around in China, the search was on for something to replace it and we prisoners had the honour of being the guinea pigs for the various ersatzes the scientific community came up with. The warder describing the new nutritional policy told us that paper pulp was guaranteed harmless and though it contained no nutritive value, it would make our *wo'tous*[2] fatter and give us the satisfying impression of bulk. The new flour mix would be no more than 30 per cent powdered paper pulp. It will go through your digestive tracts easily, he said with assurance. We know exactly how you will feel.

Sure enough, our *wo'tous* the next day were considerably bigger and we had the pleasant sensation of putting more into our stomachs. They tasted like the normal loaves, but were a bit limper in texture. We ate them without complaint. That evening I saw Ma Erh-kang, the prison doctor. A prisoner like the rest of us, he had no particular respect for most of the warders and certainly none for their medical capabilities. He told me he was worried about the ersatz.

'If I were you, Bao, I'd try to eat some fatty things,' he advised, but it was an empty thought under the circumstances.

'You're joking, Ma,' I said. 'Where in hell am I going to get fat?'

He shrugged and looked preoccupied.

'I don't know, but I don't like that stuff. It may not contain anything poisonous, but I wonder what it will do to the digestive tract. Paper absorbs moisture.'

For a while it appeared that his fears were groundless. The bigger *wo'tous* were popular with the prisoners and they seemed digestible. At the start, anyway. There was hardly any jealousy or complaint, in fact, when the Health Preservation Diet was announced a few days later. We should have been alarmed by the ominous title, though. Bao Jian Fan, as it was called in Chinese, was established especially for those prisoners who would be holding key jobs during the winter months and who in the past had earned merits by displaying a proper attitude towards labour – and whose strength would be needed for the crucial spring planting. About 30 of the 285 in our brigade won places on the list, and among them were Sun and Soong, the one we used to call 'the Stakhanovite' for his tireless enthusiasm for doing right and serving the government. The Health Preservation Diet consisted of millet flour without ersatz and a soup made from whatever vegetables could be found, often laced with horsemeat or some kind of oil. Even that diet disintegrated as the winter went on, though. After a month or so the only difference was that they had a larger portion of vegetables.

On the second day of the diet old Sun was already too embarrassed to eat his food with us in the cell, as he had done the first day. He ended his personal crisis with one dramatic and illegal gesture. When he walked back from the kitchen his painted tin mug was brimming with a soup of horsemeat, vegetables and fat. He paused long enough to make certain that everybody was watching – and then emptied his mug into our communal soup tub.

'Your health needs preserving, too,' he growled. 'You can report me if you like.'

The Stakhanovite was confused. He wasn't used to breaking the rules. No one thought he would report Sun, but he obviously didn't know what to do now.

'Don't think you're so well off, Soong,' Sun said sharply. 'Next spring they won't expect these people to work so hard, because they've had a bad winter, but guys like you and me are going to be slaving because we've had all that good food. We'll need all the help we can get.'

Soong slopped his mug into the tub. I suppose it must have been those two extra portions of fat over the next two weeks that saved our cell from having any paper-pulp deaths. By Christmas day the whole farm was in agony from what was probably one of the most serious cases of mass constipation in medical history. Sounds comical, doesn't it? It wasn't. Just as Doc Ma had predicted, the paper powder absorbed the moisture from our digestive tracts, making it progressively harder to defecate as each day passed. And painful. Men were bent double with craps. Even soapy water enemas did hardly any good, for those few who had the honour of using the single apparatus in the farm's medical inventory. I had to stick my finger up my anus and dig it out, in dry lumps, like sawdust. The prison authorities finally backed off in alarm, gave us straight mush and instructed us to drink lots of water. I never saw it personally, but we heard that many of the older and weaker ones died trying to shit their guts out. I do recall a little scene in the fields, though, when Sun and I walked by one character squatting down by the edge of the road, shaking and sweating with the effort in spite of the cold.

'Look at that,' Sun spat out with surprising rancour. 'Another one of Mao's benefits for you.'

After paper pulp flopped, someone in central planning came up with the bright idea of trying marsh water plankton. Since plankton was said to be almost 100 per cent protein, the idea seemed brilliant – in theory. They skimmed the slimy, green stuff off the swampy ponds around the camp and mixed it in with the mush either straight or dried and powdered, since it tasted too horrible to eat unaccompanied. Again, we all fell sick and some of the weaker ones died. That particular plankton, they discovered after a few autopsies, was practically unassimilable for the human body. End of plankton experiment. At length our daily ersatz became ground corn cobs, mixed in with the *wo'tou* flour. Afterwards it was adopted as the standard food supplement for the country at large. We had been pioneers.

Camp 585

One drizzly day in August a new warder I had never seen before came to the infirmary to look us over. He was dressed in a white shirt, khaki shorts and sandals, and seemed totally efficient. He took down our names and asked us about our health histories. When he had left I asked Dr Ma what his visit was all about.

'Nothing good or bad,' he replied obliquely. He often spoke in riddles – it's an old Chinese habit. The next morning the new warder was back again. This time he had that bastard Liu with him.

'The government is always concerned with your welfare,' Liu said, and I thought to myself: Here it comes. It *had* to be some sort of bad news. 'Number Three Farm is a production unit and as such has neither the means nor the time to care for the sick. For this reason the government has decided to transfer you to a place where there is proper medical care. It is called Camp 585, and it is especially designed for the needs of the sick. Now get your things ready. You are leaving immediately.'

Those of us who could walk climbed on to a truck and the rest were carried aboard. We rolled over dirt roads through the fields for several hours before drawing up in front of a roughshod hamlet of red brick and whitewashed buildings surrounded by a flat mud embankment into which was stuck a large wooden panel with the numbers 5-8-5. We clambered down and when I caught sight of the old one-armed warder I had known before, Wang, I realized that this must just be a larger version of Northern Precious Village, the dying farm.Wang remembered me perfectly well, and on the strength of our past acquaintance made me group leader of our bunch.

We spent the rest of the afternoon and evening settling in one of the whitewashed cell units, finding out about rations and generally getting acquainted. Very quickly I saw some familiar faces from Northern Precious Village and got filled in on the situation. The old place had been requisitioned, they told me, when the agronomists had found some crops that would grow well in the surrounding soil. Camp 585 was to be the new consolidation point for all the weak, crippled and aged, and not many of them felt there was any chance of getting back out alive. We were 400 in all, and we ate twice a day, mostly the extras from the other production units. That wasn't much in those days. I shuffled around in the mud of the courtyard, watching some desultory foragers over by the kitchen waste heap, depressed and feeling hopeless and abandoned. It really looked like the end of the road.

The same tiresome, pointless routine continued the next morning, still under a fine, grey drizzle. Since we had no jobs and no work norms, the only activity appeared to be waiting to eat. Some time after noon Warder Wang called me to his office.

'You're leaving,' he announced without ceremony. 'You're going back to Number Three Farm. Get your things.'

I was astonished and exhilarated. Suddenly my future seemed more possible. I didn't know it then, but I learned later that it was Wang himself who declared me undesirable for 585. It was a very conscious and pointed gesture: he meant to save my life. He knew all too well that 585 was nothing but a death farm.

My exceptional bounce back to Number Three Farm didn't work without complication, though. This time I was accepted into the infirmary with only Class C rations – exactly half what the normal workers were getting. Evidently someone in the hierarchy, probably Warder Liu, had decided that I had shown myself to be a malcontent by having refused the government's benevolent offer of medical treatment in Camp 585. It wasn't until I had written a formal letter of protest to the camp director, explaining that I had been retransferred without my consent or prior knowledge, and had always acted in good faith, that Liu relented and allowed me back in the cell on Class B rations.

'Letter of protest' may sound wildly improbable for those who do not understand the Chinese prison system or the mentality of the cadres. As I learned in Prison Number One, everybody, even a prisoner, is encouraged to speak his mind honestly and fully, for the government wants to know what goes on in a man's head. In this manner if the thoughts are erroneous or not in sync with the party line, they can be corrected. No one would have thought of preventing me from sending my letter up the chain of command. The strange, Alice-in-Wonderland world of forms must always be served. My jailers had absolute authority over my body and soul, but they were obliged to hear me out. On my side, though, it imported that I be careful with my ideology. Free speech is encouraged especially if it remains within the accepted channels.

My recovery after I returned from 585 was surprisingly rapid. I don't know whether to ascribe it to the ministrations of Dr Ma, the diet supplements of Sun and Longman, or simply fear of the death farm, but I was soon out in the fields with the others. One of the first big jobs that fell to us was to weed out the rice paddies and loosen the earth around the young shoots – the classical Chinese bent-back, straw-hatted labour that illustrates millions of prints, cigar boxes and coffee tables in the West. It was the timeless image of Asia, and I was happy to be back inside it. The greatest pleasure of working in the paddies (besides serving socialism) was catching the frogs that proliferated there. I never could understand how they could be so numerous when the past few years had been so disastrously lean, but there they were, and none of us questioned our good fortune. They weren't even particularly difficult to stalk – often they would literally jump into our laps. We would skin them on the spot and eat them raw. The system is to start with the mouth, and the head comes off with the spine. Those with greater discipline would save the meat in their mugs with a little water (at that time of year we always carried our mugs with us, stuck down in the folds of our clothes) and then dry it in the sun to make a type of jerky. Salted, they had a delicious, delicate flavour. Sun roasted them on a stick and they tasted like bacon. Later in the summer when there were more wild vegetables, we would make all kinds of stews with them.

Around wheat-threshing time I witnessed a terrible suicide. Just as we were sitting in the shade for our midday meal of soup and *wo'tous*, a prisoner in a tattered white shirt and blue pants appeared in the field next to us, running with desperate energy towards one of the big wheat-chopping machines set into the ground. Before anyone had a chance to react, or cut off the machine, he had dived down into the blades. I never knew why he did it, but it wasn't rare for prisoners to get out of the camps that way. This one ended up in pieces.

In early September, Sun let me in on something of a secret, or at least an explanation of why the cellmates had taken such good care of me when I was in the infirmary. We were working the paddies then, and it was around 3 p.m. when he ambled over to me.

'Come on Bao,' he said, 'don't knock yourself out. It won't get you anywhere. Let's have a smoke.'

Why not? There was no warder in sight, and discipline was somewhat more relaxed now that the wheat was safely harvested and the rice seemed to be all right. We settled back against the bank of one of the raised roadways that intersected the paddies, took off our straw hats, drew out our little squares of newspaper and rolled ourselves a couple of vine-leaf smokes. Sun gestured broadly out at the fields.

'Look at that, Bao, isn't that a magnificent sight?'

It was difficult to tell whether or not he was being sarcastic, for in point of fact it *was* a magnificent sight. It was a Cinemascope day with an intensely blue sky pocked with rich, billowy cloud formations. The vast series of paddies before us stretched limitlessly to the horizon with nothing breaking the geometric pattern except the one long row of acacias and poplars over by the main highway. The dikes and pathways that separated them marched along in disciplined order. Everywhere we looked there were men, bareback or in black shirts, bent to their work, impervious to the world about them, each one lost in his personal universe. There were thousands of them.

'Isn't that wonderful?' Sun asked again. 'All those people, and none of them will ever make it out, me included. Lifetime contract. You're the only one who's different, Bao. You might get out the Big Door some day. It could happen to a foreigner, but not us. You'll be the only one who can tell about it afterwards if you do. That's why we wanted to keep you alive, Bao.'

I was touched, but didn't quite feel his optimism. 'I don't know if I'll live that long, Sun.'

That wasn't theatrical pessimism on my part. Since August 1960, more than three-quarters of our brigade had died or been dispatched to Camp 585. There weren't many of us left.

'Don't you worry,' Sun said firmly, 'as long as you're here, you'll live. I can promise you that. And if you get transferred to other camps, there'll be other people who think like us. You're precious cargo, old man.'

Sun laughed and sloshed back out into the paddy.

Christmas on Strip 23

The last extraordinary experience I had at Qinghe was the Christmas mass of Father Hsia. Our teams had spent most of the month of December in miscellaneous agricultural housekeeping, such as marking boundaries for rice paddies, cleaning out irrigation ditches and cutting brush. The morning was bright and clear that Christmas Day, but the temperature was close to zero, and a force five wind was roaring down from the northwest. The eighteen men under me were laying out paddy markers on Field Strip 23, a plot of clean ploughed earth about two miles long and 120 yards wide, in which we were to mark out sixty paddies, set down the stakes and then turn it over to other teams who would set up the system of irrigation ditches. I divided the section into five teams of three each and sent the remaining three to gather scrap wood for a bonfire.

It was around 9.30 when I noticed a solitary figure approaching me across the strip. Even quite far away, I could tell from his gait that it was Hsia. The earflaps of his ragged old cotton hat danced in the wind as he hurried over to me, and his faded khaki army overcoat and black padded pants were splattered with mud. With the exaggerated politeness characteristic of him, Hsia asked me if he could have a break for a few minutes. I had nothing against that, but he knew we had a deadline for the paddy job – couldn't he wait until lunch? Embarrassed and pained, he looked down at his boots, toying absently with the red-and-white markers he still held in his mittens.

'Don't you remember what day it is today, John?' he asked me in English.

Of course. I had been thickheaded.

'Go on, old man,' I said, 'but be careful.'

He smiled gratefully and scurried away across the road and down the embankment to a dry gully where a bonfire was burning, and where he was shielded from the wind and the view of the warders. A quarter of an hour later, I saw a bicycle against the sky in the distance – a warder was on his way. I hustled over to the gully to warn Hsia.

As I looked down the embankment I saw that he was just finishing up the mass, in front of a mound of frozen earth which he had chosen as an altar. He was making the traditional gestures of priests all over the world. But his vestments here were ragged work clothes; the chalice, a chipped enamel mug; the wine, some improvised grape juice; and the host, a bit of *wo'tou* he had saved from breakfast. I watched him for a moment and knew quite well it was the truest mass I would ever see. I loped down the embankment, and when the warder passed on his bike he saw only two prisoners warming their hands.

---

[1] Labour camp east of Tianjin.
[2] Steamed corn buns, a staple food in north China.

Abdellatif Laabi

Abdellatif Laabi (born 1942) spent eight years in a Moroccan prison for 'crimes of opinion'. This is an extract from *Rue du Retour*, a memoir of his time in prison, the comradeship he found there, and his new life and rediscovery of passion, after his unexpected return to family and friends.

Extract from *Rue du Retour*

Whatever of us died in the ripples of exile
look at me now on the threshold of learning
everything amazes me
the earth
rebelling against night
pushing men
into the whirlpool of apathy
O my sad one
the lover of my powerful dreams
when will I again be able
to spell out the letters
of my rude name.

The full blast of the street. You give your hand to your wife for this first dip into the crowd.

You walk like any other of freedom's porters, oblivious of their precious cargo. You feel none too steady on your legs. Your body pitches slightly. You feel again that spray-seasoned dizziness which heralds seasickness as the unsettled gulls throw out their eerie cry in every direction.

A warm wind smelling of seaweed and the musk of pollen overwhelms you, stings your nostrils, your eyelids and collects in every pore of your face. You open your hand, seize a fistful of the odour and put it in your pocket. Sleep-walking in daylight, you do not distinguish passers-by too well. The crowd's still in a state of nebulous motion where

hundreds of eyes are fixed on you, hostile, lazy, bewildered.
They ceaselessly measure you from head to foot, swarm
around the nape of your neck, survey the whole length of
your backbone, spin round, attack your stomach and then
seize and pull the hairs of your beard. Hostile, lazy,
bewildered eyes. They undress you as if they wanted to
examine this body of yours, see into the depths of your soul,
follow the contours and shape of this pain with which you
are assumed to be tattooed even in your most intimate
places.

You try not to meet these looks, to make yourself very
small in your wife's hand and in your new civilian clothes.
But those very clothes accentuate your incongruity. For
even though they are dark blue and soberly cut, you think
they are too revealing, that they mould you too closely, that
they give you a Sunday-best, peacockish air. You still do not
wear them as you used to wear your prison uniform. The
brown cloth uniform in winter, the striped canvas in
summer, yours and those of your fellow prisoners were a
unifying force. It was the origin of the feeling which took
hold of you when you sat down in the exercise yard with
your back to the wall and settled down to look at your
comrades as they walked around. Their clothing no longer
held your attention. You could see them better, smile at the
temperament of each one which revealed itself in the
simplest way in the world – in his demeanour, his way of
holding his arms, the theatrical gestures which
accompanied his speech and his automatic comings and
goings.

A blast from a car horn puts an end to your daydream,
and your wife pulls you firmly back to let a car pass. You
discover the aggressive round of traffic. The cars go at an
abnormal speed. Whirling and scattering in every direction,
they remind you of the dodgems in fairs of the dim and
distant past. The street is like a battlefield. Pedestrians and
motorists are given over to a war of strategies and attrition.
He who manoeuvres best is the one who gets first place in
the opposing lines.

You get across as best you can, rejoin the mass which stretches along the pavement of the great avenue. You still aren't managing to look straight ahead, to well and truly meet those eyes, and challenge them to find another object for their curiosity.

You lift up your head to cast a look over the whole perspective of the avenue. The large buildings reassume one by one their places in your revitalized memory. Bank, Post Office, railway station, Courts of Justice and right at the bottom a minaret, like a watchtower lording it over these new arrivals. You can't remember whether this minaret used to be there or at least if it used to be so clearly visible. It is possible that the avenue has been widened, that some buildings have been demolished to improve the perspective and to bring about this special realignment which is desirable as a faithful reflection of the other realignments which have been created in your country during your absence. As ever your attention is especially focused on the examples of colonial-moorish architecture. It is here that Lyautey had succeeded in imparting to his urban engineers a moral which had proved useful elsewhere. *Show your power so as not to have to use it* was the motto. Public buildings had to inspire in each citizen the feeling of the power of the state and of its continuity. No capricious decorations which could be interpreted as weakness in the System, but a reminder that this state was a product of a grafting and that in order that this graft should take well it was necessary to preserve something of the original plant, even if only at the level of the local material, local colour, of a graphic symbolism whose significance had become more and more hazy for the natives themselves.

In spite of that, you feel a tightening in your heart at seeing again those ambiguous buildings which have successfully survived so many social cataclysms including your own without anyone ever thinking of questioning their use and their continued place in the scenery of everyday life. The world is like that, you say to yourself. Men are like that, these products of successive graftings who struggle for the whole of their lives to reinstate a space of original purity even though this effort pushes them even deeper into multiplicity.

Translated by Jacqueline Kaye

Ala Mehrzad

Dr Ala Mehrzad is an Iranian refugee who was imprisoned for five years for his political beliefs and activities. He now lives in Britain and is rebuilding his life as a doctor.

Dr Mehrzad worked with Sonja Linden (Writer-in-Residence of the Medical Foundation) to write this piece.

Words Can Save Lives

It was during the cold days of the winter of 1982, in Iran. The whole country was under the harsh pressure of a cruel tornado of political violence, with mass arrests and continuous executions. I was in solitary confinement and under interrogation. My cell was in Section 207 in a special part of hell known as Evin prison. It was like a forgotten island in the depths of that netherworld inhabited by political prisoners. Death bats flew over our heads, signalling what might lie at the end of those terrifying days and nights. My cell was dimly lit and its walls were made of cement, whose harsh ugliness seemed to add to the bitterness of that space. There was a small window in the ceiling, but it was impossible to see out of it.

I was only twenty years old and I felt like a lost person in a land of dwarfs and devils. I could see neither stars in the sky, nor the setting and rising of the sun, I could hear no natural sounds, no singing of birds or falling of rain. All I could hear were the angry, psychotic screams of the guards and the grief-stricken weeping of the prisoners. There were no smiles, there were no colours; it was entirely a world of grey. I could not even see myself, because there was no mirror. The shadow of death was very close, it hung like a thick fog, just within my reach. Yet even death was unimportant compared with the much more potent issue of how to prevent myself giving away information which might result in the arrest and death of others. I tried singing or reciting poems aloud, I tried reviewing my life and experiences, but nothing could assuage the fear and terror of that possibility.

One night I was brought into the interrogation room and ordered to tell the truth about my activities and to name every person and place I could. I was unable to see my interrogator because I was blindfolded. He was standing very close to me. I sensed that he was short. There was something nasty, repulsive in his voice. My life and future were in his hands. I felt something in my throat. My hands were clammy. I wanted to shout out loud for help, but I could not. I wanted to die, but I could not. I was there, with a pen and some sheets of paper for questions and answers. I sighed slowly, and pushed my blindfold up a bit to see the paper. I remembered taking exams at school and university, and how I always used to lift up my paper before I began, to read what other people had written on the desk flap. Unconsciously I found myself doing the same thing. I saw some writing on the desktop and recognized it as two lines from a famous poem:

These days, which are more bitter than poison, shall pass
And days which are sweet as sugar will follow.

I read these lines like a thirsty man stranded in the desert, afflicted by harsh sand winds. They brought a chunk of sweetness to my dry and bitter mouth. They were like a refuge for me in which to rest a while. 'Do not believe this situation will last for ever,' they said. 'You may see a better tomorrow.'

That extract from a poem, scrawled by another prisoner, was very short and consisted of very few words, but its impact was enormous. Do not underrate the power of the written word. Words can save lives, they can give hope, they can restore life.

Rad Baan

Rad John Charles Herbert Baan was once a well-known singer in Kuwait. When the Iraqis invaded in 1990 he found himself thrown into prison on the trumped-up charge of stealing his own car. The intelligence agents who arrested him wanted the Mercedes 500 for themselves.

He spent the following five and a half years stuck in the maw of the Iraqi prison system – two of them under sentence of death for insulting Saddam Hussein and his mother. Rad had been secretly filmed referring to the Iraqi dictator as 'a son of a bitch'.

Despite extensive torture, Rad, born in 1959, refused to succumb to the brutality around him, making a point instead of always trying to be a 'gentleman and a nice guy'. Freed when his family paid a hefty bribe to a corrupt Iraqi official to have his name added to an amnesty list on Saddam Hussein's birthday, Rad escaped across the border into Saudi Arabia. He now lives as a refugee on a north London council estate – unwelcome back in Kuwait because his mother was Iraqi. His survival he sometimes finds difficult to believe.

Testimony

I lived five and half years in horror. In the end I was not thinking about beating or torture, but when they were going to come for me with the rope; how I would fall, to the left or the right, and what the pain in my neck would be like.

I made it because I believe in God. I almost lost my faith in prison but God gave me strength. And my body was in good shape too. And maybe my name also helped. I was called John Charles Herbert after my grandfather, a British army officer in Baghdad. In prison it made me different. The other prisoners always treated me as a guest in their country. And the senior officers knew they might be able to make some money out of me so the guards had to be a little bit more careful.

123

I was born in Baghdad but brought up in Kuwait, where my father worked for an airline. As a young man, I used to do parties, private parties. When people get married, in Gulf society, they make a special party for women and a special party for men. I used to do parties for women.

Money matters were very good. Kuwait was a very luxurious society. If you are working there it is very easy to get cars, a nice house, servants. And you could travel. If you have two dinars in the pound, well, I used to earn 450 dinars for playing say from 8 p.m. until midnight. I would get that every night, working maybe three or four months with parties every night. I was doing very good. I had four cars and servants who would even open my cigarettes for me. If I came to London, it was Mayfair, the Dorchester or whatever, casinos and luxury cars – usually Bentleys. Don't say first class. It had to be deluxe.

My luck was that I was in Kuwait when the Iraqis invaded. About a week after they arrived we were getting hungry – the soldiers took all the food – so I went out to find bread. I was driving my Mercedes and they stopped me, three security men, no uniforms, just ordinary clothes. They asked some questions, then they said I had stolen the car. It was as easy as that. They wanted it for themselves, so I was called a thief and taken to prison in Basra.

There were some Filipino and Indian servants there who had been arrested for looting and when the Iraqis heard me speak English to them they took me back to Kuwait to work as an interpreter. Saddam had sent some big officers to stop the looting and they were arresting a lot of people. I got a lot of beatings there.

Then just before the Allies attacked I was taken back to Iraq, to al-Hartha prison about ten miles outside Basra. We were thirteen in a room for two or three. We were only there a short time before we heard about the cease-fire on the radio. The next morning there was machine-gun fire. The Iraqi prisoners thought it was American paratroopers but instead it was people against the regime liberating the prison.

I walked with the other prisoners towards Basra. We had been told that Saddam was dead, but as we reached the town the Republican Guards attacked. I tried to hide in several houses but the shelling was too heavy. Some of the civilian people thought I was a spy for the government – nobody trusted anybody. My feet were badly injured by flying glass so in the end I gave myself up to the army.

An officer who felt sorry for me took me by jeep to a highway and just told me to go. A family living close by took me and sheltered me for two days but they were frightened. Iraqi soldiers were still searching for people who had taken part in the uprising.

I heard that it was impossible to go over the border to Kuwait so decided to go to Baghdad. I went back to the army and this time the same soldiers started beating me with their rifles, kicking and shouting.

They took me to a college in the middle of Basra next to al-Saad Square where they used to train oil-tanker crews. I was pushed into a big hall where there were about 1,200 of us in a space for maybe 200. There was shit and water on the floor up to the ankles, dying people, people with bullet wounds. I asked one man how long he had been there and he said nine days. It was unbelievable.

I stood for as long as possible but eventually I had to sit in the shit to rest my legs. Then the next day they pushed us all out into the courtyard and began questioning people one by one. They beat people – the soldiers didn't talk, they just kept beating – then a senior officer would flick his hand if he decided the person being questioned should die, and that person would be put up against the wall and shot. The bodies were thrown out on the street for the dogs to eat.

I thought it was the end of the world. I remember one prisoner in an army officer's uniform went to the man ordering the killing and started to beg. The officer just snarled and waved his hand. He was shot immediately.

There was a car in the compound – a white Chevrolet with a woman inside whom the officers were taking it in turns to rape. She was laughing as though she was crazy.

God knows what happened to her. I love people but at times like that you don't think of what other people are suffering. You are concentrating instead on yourself, how to avoid being beaten, what to say when it's your time for questioning, what it's like to die. My back was black and blue from being hit but all I could think about was staying alive.

When they realized I was a civilian from Kuwait, I was taken to a school where I was held five days blindfolded without food and water. I was surprised that I was still alive at the end. Then I was taken to Basra police station, where I spent three months wondering what was going to happen to me.

In the end I was taken to court. All the Kuwaiti charges had been dropped, but the judge said I could only be released on bail. It was 750 dinars. I lied and said there were people in Iraq who would stand bail for me and back at the police station I tried to come to a deal with the police officers.

That evening a man walked into the police station to enquire about another case and I recognized him as someone who had worked at my mother's factory. He stood bail and I was released.

He then arranged for me to go to Baghdad, where I went to the Red Cross for help but they had no solution for me. For more than a month I was free in the city but I had no papers, no money, nothing. So I had to borrow money and when I couldn't repay it, the lender complained against me and I was kept four months in a police station.

We were nearly a hundred people in a cell for ten. There was never enough to eat or drink. I heard that in one cell a man furthest from the door died of thirst. That's in a country with two big rivers. It was a very brutal regime – the officers would come in and beat us around the head with heavy electric cables.

Each morning a sergeant would arrive and read out a list of names. These were people sentenced to Dore Tebidir. It means something like Behaviour Programme and was for quite serious matters like stealing cars or raping. Those whose names were read out would go around and say goodbye to the rest of us very sadly. Ten would leave and maybe three would come back – all disabled.

They would be taken to the police ministry, where they were locked in dog cages and beaten three times a day. The police minister's bodyguards would beat to kill, using pipes, a spanner, anything.

While I was in the cell, a Kurd came up to me. He was a journalist and he said once I was released, he knew someone who would smuggle me out of the country. I know the Kurdish people, they are against Saddam, so I trusted him. But these were Kurdish people who worked for Saddam's intelligence.

They took me north to the town of Mosul, from where they were supposed to smuggle me out in a lorry. There we waited chatting in a hotel while the arrangements were made. In those days I used to drink a lot, I was suffering, and I used to talk. At some point Saddam's face came on the TV in the hotel room and I swore, calling him a son of a bitch.

I didn't think anything of it. Anyway, the plan changed. They said I couldn't go by lorry, it was too dangerous. After a while it seemed they were pushing me not to go so I decided to return to Baghdad to see if there was anyone else who could get me out. As I had no identification with me, I went to the security to ask them for permission to stay in a hotel. It was a crazy thing to do; it was the drink.

They were suspicious of my Kuwaiti accent, lack of papers and foreign name, and asked what I was doing in Mosul. I said I had wanted some fresh air from the city. But they didn't believe me, and arrested me. I was so frightened I could barely stand.

From Mosul I was taken to Baghdad – to al-Mansour, the intelligence headquarters. There they took my clothes away and gave me pyjamas and the number 887. They said my name was finished. That first week I was beaten every day – prisoners called it washing. They want to break you down.

Then they tried to persuade me to work for them. They told me I was under sentence of death for insulting Saddam Hussein and his mother while in the hotel room in Mosul. Of course I denied it, so they showed me the video. I had been secretly filmed.

Somewhere they had also found a cassette of me singing in big houses, so they knew I was very close to the Kuwaiti royal family. One of them said, 'We can close this file but for everything there is a price. You know people from the Gulf, high-class people. You could deliver car bombs for us. We will put you in a better situation than you were when you were in Kuwait, with servants, cars, money or whatever you want.'

He asked what guarantee I could give them that I would do what I was ordered, and when I said I didn't know, he suggested that I get my mother from Kuwait to live in Baghdad. They would give her a villa to live in.

I told him my sisters, who are all married to Kuwaitis, would never allow her to make such a trip. From that moment on, an X was put against my name and the beatings and torture got much worse. My leg was broken twice – deliberately. They pulled my toenails out, and gave me electric shocks, and all the time they were beating me. This went on for weeks.*

I was in a room with fifty other people and each morning they would come and read out a list of numbers. Those were the people they took for hanging. Every morning for two and a half years I woke up waiting to hear 887. At first I couldn't sleep. Then after about a month and a half I started sleeping a bit and after four months I slept normally.

Thank God I survived, but what I went through is never far away.

---

*But their own people they treat much worse. One guard said to me, 'If I don't beat them, they won't respect me.' It's a barbaric culture. The people there have lost their mercy.

EXILE

Those fleeing persecution lose everything: their friends, their family, their home. A new country may be a refuge but it is still a foreign place and so much has been left behind.

Babek

I was always under threat. I couldn't stay in touch with my family. The regime said to me that if they arrested me again they would kill me, so I decided to escape. I stayed in a few places and then I ended up in the UK. I came here because my brother was here. I was always in pain, in heart and mind and body. I felt hopeless, homeless, like I was drowning. I wanted to talk to my brother and I didn't want to. I didn't want to tell him, to torture him. To tell him about how our brother had died and how I had held him in my arms. He was asking and I was telling him nice things. Because when you tell someone about these things, you are passing on the horror of it for them to have as well.

I used to think that in this country, I am not getting anything new. My memories and my childhood are in my own country. Once, I went for a walk and it was raining and it mixed with the dust on the road and it smelled like it used to in my homeland with my people. I will always feel like that. I will always miss my country.

I thought that people would be selfish but that was not true. They did care, doctors did listen to my words and my pain. I wanted to tell my father these things, that you can find gold anywhere, but he died before I could tell him. He died when I was here and my family didn't tell me for a long time. They knew that if I found out, I would come back and it would be dangerous for me. I was here when he died.

At first when I came I thought that I could not survive, I am full of misery. I felt guilty at first because I was here and I even thought about killing myself. Then I thought that I could kill some of these frightening nightmares in my life and mind. Why should I climb the mountain all the time when there is an even road? And I needed to be able to live to tell people about what has happened, to deliver a message. I am a witness.

Maria Jastrzebska

This poem appeared in a magazine called *GEN* (Issue 12/13: *Refugee Women in Britain*), which is no longer published. We were unable to find Maria Jastrzebska and would very much like to hear from her.

The Good Immigrant

for good people
everywhere

The good immigrant is like any other good person
Born or living on the wrong side of the world
Who stands a good chance of being accepted
Into the right places
Into mainstream channels
Along cosy corridors
The good immigrant has been taken aside and told as much
Probably a little confidential chat here
A whisper there a nod a certain understanding
Or a look
But at the same time
This good person's always in danger
Of being unexpectedly kicked out.

Now it goes without saying
That there are some conditions
Which have to be fulfilled
If you want to be accepted.
You are supposed to be white or light
Or practising the right religion
To change your name or to have lost your accent
Or if you can't do that
Then in some other way
To have lost all trace of the past
Or of your heart
So it doesn't embarrass anyone.

You have to bend to blend in
With your new surroundings
To fit in your place
To lower your eyes
Or if you can't do that
Then learn to lower your expectations.
It is important that you know
How to curb your anger
Especially when you are a woman
Hold back your laughter
Only letting out correct amounts of it
In appropriate situations
And you must cover up your strength
As well as your exhaustion
Except for when it shows you're working
Twice as hard as everybody else.

But most of all
You've got to be prepared to show
You're not like all the rest
That you're more cultured more adjusted
Balanced more willing less extreme
And that you know how to remain silent
About what is done to others.
If you can manage this
There is a good chance of you being accepted
But there is also a danger
A badly growing danger
You won't want in.

Ediba-Bakira Kapic

I was born in Stolac, Bosnia and Herzegovina in 1976 and I lived
there for sixteen years. I was in Stolac for the first five months of
war in 1992, and then I went to Croatia to live there as a refugee.
My mother joined me there later, but my father stayed in Stolac,
because he wanted to and because he is an orthopaedic surgeon,
and he was needed. My father was imprisoned by Croats in 1993
and was kept in various concentration camps for thirteen months.
During this period, I had come to London, as the Croats did not
want me in their country and didn't allow me to go to school as I
am a Muslim. When I came to London, I missed my family so
much, especially my dad, whom I didn't know anything about.
This piece of prose was written because I wanted to show to people
around me how it feels when you are seventeen, alone at the gate
on Terminal Two. I have two brothers, and they are both in
Sarajevo, and so are my mum and dad now. I am doing physics,
chemistry and maths A level.

Ediba returned to join her family in September 1996. They have not
been able to return to their home town. She is now studying for a
degree in English and English literature.

Terminal Two

Lights, different colours of lights. I am supposed to follow
the arrows, little flashy arrows that say 'way out'. Way out
of what? To where? It doesn't give the hope, just another
question. I am pulling my life behind me, squeezing tightly
to my identity, paper with my name, me. I don't want to get
lost in this crowd of faces, voices and bodies. It is me here,
standing, waiting for a rescue from the unknown. It must be
years since the hand stamped the passport and the voice
said, 'Welcome to Britain.' Why am I still here?
     The luggage is spinning around me, people pushing
through, going back to something, maybe even someone.

And I am, as always, going in the opposite direction, leaving all I ever cared for behind. They even stopped staring at me, the picture of a lost face with dried lines of tears coming down, it has become too common. Please, will someone find me? I am waiting, ready to give all my love and gratitude to the first smile that meets me. You don't know, you'll never know. No more tears and screams. Now just fear. My heart is going back by itself and the legs can't even make a step. I am supposed to go through. Please be there. Let me hug you. Maybe you'll smell like my mother, like my father, maybe even that first little flower that comes out of February snow. Maybe the door will open and the smell of white coffee will tickle my nose.

No one?

I have my bravery down in my throat, I am ready to swallow it, lose it for ever. Can I follow you? You look like the person who knows where she is going, and is going there with purpose. Share it with me, will you? The feeling of coming home. There isn't a plane in this world that would take me to the town too small even for an aeroplane track. The town with the wild blue river, four mountains and those sixteen years of me in it. I'll close my eyes tightly, make a wish, and when I open them, it is not going to be Terminal Two I see, but that tree under which I wrote my first poem.

It looks like I left the magic behind as well. It is still Terminal Two. I'll wait. A century more, and then I'll go back, face the failure once more and finally admit to myself that the geography means nothing to me any more.

Wherever I go, I'll be anything but wanted.

Is that you? Get me out of here. This place doesn't like me. You know, now I'll love you for ever. It was easy, wasn't it? You only had to be there for a moment and now I'll carry you with me my whole life. Thank you. For one moment of safety in this wild storm.

Alfredo Cordal

Alfredo Cordal (born 1941) worked as a journalist in Chile in charge of a magazine for the workers in the factories along the coast of the country. He also worked as a freelance journalist covering cultural news in the Press Department of Channel 13 Catholic University. At the time of the military coup in September 1973, he was suspended from work and underwent interrogation by the military for five months. In February 1974, he managed to get to Buenos Aires, Argentina, where he was treated for acute paranoia, together with other Chilean friends. Many of the psychologists and Argentine friends who helped at that time are still missing. He came to the UK as a refugee in 1974, before the coup in Argentina in 1975. He now lives in London and works as a journalist and Spanish teacher. He has been writing plays and poems and doing readings of his poetry for Amnesty International, Praxis and other human rights organizations.

Exile Is an Island of No Return

Exile is a faraway island
surrounded entirely by memories,
and races of all colour find themselves anchored there
compelled to seek the history of their countries
in the labyrinth of libraries,
or accumulated in museums and in secret undergrounds.
All the inhabitants of the island are strangers
who neither look at each other nor speak to one another
and they walk numbed along the jigsaw-like streets
where always one piece is missing
or there are pieces which don't fit or are the same,
and where all the addresses a person is seeking
end up always in a derelict house . . .
On the island night comes in the middle of the day
and Time is a train always late
and running along that golden rail

which crosses the clock's face from East to West.
There is a legend which says that once one is there
one never leaves the island alive,
and those that have come to live on the island
have forgotten why they have come
or when they have arrived at the island's ports.
In fact, all the inhabitants on the island become blind
and can only see in their dreams and nightmares.
And they spend the rest of their days
looking for a treasure that lies hidden down in the hole
where Alice fell down chasing her rabbit.
And this island is England perhaps . . . ?
No. It's only this planet exiled in the universe.

Liu Hongbin

Liu Hongbin is an ex-client of the Foundation who first came in 1991. He is the author of two collections of poems, *The Dove of the East* (1983) and *An Iron Circle* (1992).

He was born in 1962 in Shandong, China. His father was killed by the communist regime during the Cultural Revolution. Liu Hongbin was expelled from school for disgracing China and frequently questioned, harassed and detained by the security police for his literary and political activities. During the Tiananmen Square demonstrations in 1989, he posted up four of his poems around the square and shortly afterwards was forced into exile and came to Britain. His poems have been broadcast and published outside China but not a single line of his verse has been allowed to appear there. He went back to China to see his mother in 1997 but was again arrested, detained and expelled. He has been banned from ever returning. Stephen Spender described him as a 'gifted and serious poet'.

The Unfamiliar Customs House

Nightmares waylaid me. I could hardly make a declaration to the customs officer. I had become a smuggler, dealing in nightmares. I was once again in exile.

When I took up my pen for the first time to write poetry I felt exiled from the ordinary world; then I was only a teenager. My exile was a voluntary one.

The night in London is becoming damper. Sound flutters its wings hovering in the air. The lighted cigarette in my hand is like a red eye suffering from sleeplessness.

The sky of the square still seems to me like a bloody, messy wound. My frozen tongue has become alive. I want to speak. The way I came is broken by the wind; the way back is muddy with anxiety. Paths beneath my feet run in all directions in the confused moonlight.

In that home where my childhood is stored, the mirror

had forgotten its owner. Nobody there will turn on the table lamp to lift up the night. Books in the bookcase still have my fingerprints, which have gone cold between the pages. The hanging lamp no longer tenderly gazes down at the bed. The dust of time has buried all the nightmares and all the love. The windows which let in sunlight have gone blind. Is there any green mould secretly crawling over the uncarpeted floor?

In another place Mother, through her glasses, fixes her eyes on the only photo of myself as a child, expecting my mischievous footsteps.

I want to go back; I must go back. The way swallowed up in the night has not yet come into sight. Night is like many rocks gathering to block my way back. Let the rock of the night crash into me.

Taslima Nasrin

Taslima Nasrin (born 1962) is a doctor and writer from Bangladesh. Following death threats against her by Islamic extremists accusing her of blasphemy and 'conspiracy against Islam' and the banning, in July 1993, by the Bangladesh authorities, of her book *Lajja (Shame)*, she was forced to leave her country. She went back in 1998 to be with her mother who was ill, and was still under threat. When her mother died in early 1999, she resumed living in exile in Sweden.

Siberia in My Soul

A year has passed and I am one year older, but the new year brought no promise nor hope of freedom. Exile has no limits: how long shall I spend the life of a stranger in a foreign land? I see no reason to live in hope of tomorrow.

If someone gave me a single wish, I would answer without a thought: I want to go back to my homeland, Bangladesh. So many years have passed since I left my home. So many years since I last looked on her beautiful face. Sometimes I think I'll go crazy. To those who judge me from outside, I should be happy, content. I don't have to worry about food, clothes and shelter like most of the people back home. I don't have to run for my life any more. There is no fatwa nor demonstrations against me. And no spontaneous flow of writing in my life any more.

There are so many caring, friendly people around me here. But still I cannot say I am happy. I've been uprooted from the very soil where I was born and grew up to be myself. Europe: 'the land of dreams' for so many. But what am I here? A rootless person in this alien soil, no sense of belonging. Just another plastic plant in a painted pot. No flowers bloom, even the buds wither away before their time.

Deep in my soul I still have the urge to create, once more to bring forth the flowers. I want to write again. But for the last year I could write nothing but poems. Poems born from the tears and sighs of my depressed soul. I could describe only my cravings to be a bird and fly back to my beloved Bangladesh. I remember how, in winter, birds from cold, distant lands like Siberia would make their long flight to Bangladesh in search of warmth and sunlight. I too was caught in the wintry coldness of imprisonment in my country when the fatwa was announced against me, when they put a price on my head. It was Europe that gave me shelter and saved my life. I can never forget its warm generosity.

But still my heart craves to return. To start my life as a writer again in my old familiar surroundings, among my own people. To sit behind my old writing desk, pen in hand once more. Will Bangladesh remain my eternal Siberia?

Fax Sent to Meredith

Dear Meredith,

I am in grave danger. At any time fundamentalists will kill me. My lawyers have decided to go to high court for bail day after tomorrow. I don't know what will happen. Fundamentalists declared more prize money for my head than before. Govt are against me. So I have no hope to escape from this dangerous situation. All mullahs are now in street. They are continuously demanding my death sentence. Govt are helping them. I wanted shelter in any Ambassy. But they did not give shelter. Now if you want to get me alive, you please inform your govt and create pressure to our govt by them for withdrawal of the case against me and to give police protection to me. If you can this, only then I can live. Otherwise I have to die. They must kill me. They have decided they will kill me to save the Islam. Meredith please save me.

Love, Taslima Nasrin. 13.6.94.

I am not safe inside the jail even. Mullahs are everywhere. You try to give me political asylum in your country. If I stay here, they must kill me.

Bertolt Brecht

Bertolt Brecht (1898–1956) was born in Augsburg, Germany. He lived through the rise of Hitler and Nazism and during this time his highly political work was often censored. He went into exile in 1933, first to Denmark and later to the USA. After the war he returned to Europe and in 1949 helped establish the Berliner Ensemble theatre company in East Berlin, where he lived until his death. He is regarded as one of the most important playwrights of the twentieth century.

Emigrant's Lament

I earned my bread and ate it just like you.
I am a doctor; or at least I was.
The colour of my hair, the shape of my nose
Cost me my home, my bread and butter too.

She who for seven years had slept with me
My hand upon her lap, her face against my face
Took me to court. The cause of my disgrace:
My hair was black. So she got rid of me.

But I escaped at night time through a wood
(For reasons of my mother's ancestry)
To find a country that would be my host.

Yet when I asked for work it was no good
You are impertinent, they said to me.
I'm not impertinent, I said: I'm lost.

Translated by Edith Roseveare

Adnan

Adnan, born in 1973, and his family were forced out of their home in central Bosnia by their Croat neighbours and fled to the Muslim-held town of Zenica. There, Adnan's work as an interpreter for visiting Western journalists gave rise to suspicions that he was a British spy, and once again he was forced to flee. He made his way alone to London, where he now works as an interpreter for the Medical Foundation for the Care of Victims of Torture. The unexpected death of his mother was a devastating reminder of everything he had been forced to leave behind.

Testimony

When my mother died it was unbearable. I had just got back from an air show watching Spitfires and Hurricanes – one hangover from the war is an interest in all things military – when the phone went. I had been very quiet all day but I didn't expect something like this to happen. It was my younger brother calling me from Zenica.

He asked me if my girlfriend was there and I said she was. I knew something was wrong and thought maybe my grandmother had died. He said, 'Mum is sick.' I asked if she was still alive and he said, 'No.'

I just started crying like mad. It was the worst news I have heard in my life. She was only 46 years old. Then my brother asked me if I could come – they would delay the funeral for me – but I hadn't got a passport. Anyway I couldn't – I've applied for political asylum and you lose your case if you return to your home country.

When I put the phone down the sense of powerlessness was overwhelming. She was the one who gave me life and saved all our lives when the Croats with balaclavas came to the house and started shooting. She went out and pleaded with them to let us live. The minimum I could do was attend her funeral.

I was completely lost, smaller than the smallest particle in the world. I felt I had let the whole family down. I couldn't keep in constant touch because they were not on the phone where they were living and I didn't write regular letters. Now I was never going to speak to her again.

She had what we call a multiple brain stroke, brought on by stress, neurosis and hardship of life. The worst thing is that she had the first stroke two weeks before she died but nobody told me. She was taken to hospital paralysed down one side and unable to talk, but they didn't want to worry me. They didn't want me to try to return home. They think it's better if I stay in Britain.

The guilt is always there. I should have done more to support them but I have been studying in Britain and didn't have the money to send home. But it was pure selfishness. They were struggling and I should have got a job.

My mother was the backbone of the family; the optimist, the morale raiser, the one with the real strength. My father is a great man but he needs a push. She spoke to us. If I wanted something I always spoke to her first. That was the system. Once you had persuaded her, it was done.

All the big moves in my family she initiated. She generated ideas. When she decided we were going to build a house, she sat down and designed it and it was built. There was one room – we called it the classical room – full of Louis XVI furniture that was bought in Belgrade. Another room was the Turkish room with thick carpets and Arab wall coverings. It was unconventional, but exactly how she wanted it.

As a youngster, I didn't know we were Muslims. Both my parents were good communists. My mother was poor and had a good social conscience. They met when she got a job as an assistant in a shop my father managed. She was very good looking with long dark hair and he said, 'I want you for a night – or a life.'

In 1992 when the war started I was a student at Sarajevo University doing American studies. The siege put an end to that but because I spoke some English, I began working as an interpreter for the journalists who visited central Bosnia.

The main British base was only a couple of miles away from where we lived in Vitez but even so things got steadily worse for the Muslims in the area. In April 1993 it all came to a head – on 16 April to be precise.

The previous evening I had walked through town and seen many, many Croat soldiers. I asked a Croat friend what was happening and he said, 'Go back home and be quiet. Just stay home.'

We knew that something was going to happen but we didn't think it would be too extreme. I went home and told my mother there was nothing we could do. All routes out of town were blocked.

At about four the following morning it started. I heard explosions that I knew were mortars, then small-arms fire and machine guns. I learned later that was the Muslims being massacred at Ahmici, a small village just outside Vitez.

We lived on a hill and we could see houses on fire on the other side of town, then the houses closer and closer to us started burning. The sound of the roofs falling in was horrible.

We were all crying. My mother said: 'It's going to be all right, we'll survive. Just let them take what they want.' She was trying to comfort my sister, who was seven, and my thirteen-year-old-brother. We were sheltering in the basement when a number of shots were fired at the house. They were armour-piercing rounds, which hit the boiler and some of the pipes.

Then people outside started shouting my father's name, saying, 'Come out, dirty Muslim, come out! We know you have soldiers there.' I got on the phone to call my friend, whose father was a big shot in the HDZ [the main Croat political party]. He said, 'Whatever happens, run away. They will kill all the males.'

My father stood there mute, then my mum said, 'I'm going to open the door.' She called, 'Don't shoot, don't shoot!' But as soon as she started opening it, they fired. It was pure luck that saved her. The bullets passed about 20 cm from her body. With the door open she shouted, 'Take whatever you want. We have nothing to hide. Just don't kill us.'

They said, 'Shut up, dirty bitch! We don't want you, we want your husband.'

I came out waving my UN press card to see four of them – all from Jokeri, a special unit of the HVO [the Bosnian Croat militia]. Their insignia was a joker playing card. They specialized in terror, and they all had balaclavas on.

I said, 'I'm with the UN, I'm not a soldier. I have no weapons.' One of them took my card and threw it on the ground then removed his balaclava. I was shocked to see it was one of our neighbours called Cicin, one of the worst animals, a psycho, a criminal.

I said, 'We are all neighbours, I come to your café. You know me.' My sister used to play with his daughter, for God's sake. My family stood there, hugging and crying, and I guess they took pity on us. My mother said, 'Come and have a coffee,' but they replied, 'We don't want your coffee' and left.

After that, other Croat neighbours hid us until we could get across to Zenica. There my mother coped as best she could but a large part of our lives had been wiped out. Now she has gone too. I never expected not to see her again. I miss her very much. Despite having shelter and refuge, exile is harder than I ever imagined.

Babek

'I Dream of Stars' is Babek's response to *Captured Voices.*

I Dream of Stars

Last night
I dreamt of stars
I dreamt of a widower
I was dreaming of a little child drowning in his blood,
An old mother broken in her heart

I dreamt of sad hearts
of tired hands
and I was dreaming of the old man's never-ending story
of the loss of his son
sitting quietly and digging the earth with his eyes
searching for his lost treasure.

I dreamt and I read all night,
now I call days nights as well
still I dream of dreaming
And dreaming of the unfinished story

After all I dug out the deep buried memories, painful times
and hard past. I laughed, I read and I cried for them. I
travelled to the lost past with a body released from pain, and
thought about the fighter mind, the tired and lost refugee.

What was I and what happened to me? In the middle of
the dusty passage of life I could see hands.

Thirteen years ago those hands found me. They showed
me the way. One was stroking my soul and the other putting
medicine on my wounds. All these friends showed me the
road of hope, how to fight and how to succeed.

A small room became a house of hope for lost refugees.
As one of the first few refugees who were treated by those
kind hands, I could see the shining stars. The little spark in

the heart of London was shining for the future. I knew for sure this little room in a short time was going to become a palace of hope for those tortured by the hands of politics and barbaric and cruel regimes all over the world. I knew these bright stars would blind those cruel eyes.

Drops became an ocean and joined the storm power, power of understanding and caring people.

A new power called the Medical Foundation for the Care of Victims of Torture was born. They listened to the story of a drop from the ocean.

In 1985 I escaped from a country torn apart by the vultures of politics and burnt by a mad war. As a teacher I had a war too. War against those who were sacrificing young and old people for their own interest, to fill their pocket with the outcome of the war and sit on the godfather's seat of power.

I was opposed to all their crimes against humanity. I was awakening my young, poor and hungry people's minds against this war. So naturally I became a criminal in the eyes of the government. I was arrested and tortured physically and tortured in mind and heart. Now some time after being tortured the pain in my body has eased, but the pain in my mind still has not left me alone. When I left my desecrated country, I had no other gifts for friends and yet unknown friends, but a world of sorrows and sad stories from those behind bars and those behind borders. Like so many people who lost their family or the dearest in their lives, I lost mine too. My brother was one of those who were tortured and died. He was sacrificed for his love for his people. I witnessed the torture of my other, younger brother. If you can imagine such pain, it was as if a sharp heated nail passes through your eyes and finds a way to the heart. I have seen other friends tortured in barbaric ways by irons, with cigarettes, lashed, broken arms, torn mouths, drilled eyes and knees. I was thinking, How am I going to survive? How am I going to forget this mental pain, and forget these memories?

As a teacher I wanted always to be a student, so found

another place to learn more about humanity and love more, humans who care for those suffered ones, the Medical Foundation.

It was in this place I learnt the greatest lesson in my life. They showed me the way of how to survive, and once they dressed my wounded body and soul then they gave me the power of life. They gave power to my tongue. They called every single star a sun. They gave me hope of brightness for my darkest night.

Now I do not escape from anybody, but I have not forgotten my people's enemy. Now I have learnt my lesson. Now I have found another way of fighting. I have to stay alive. I have to shine as a witness in the heart of history. I have to be a voice for those behind bars and straighten my hands to hold the hands of all those friends in black Africa, the Middle East, Latin America and in any part of the world that is behind bars of torture. I want to give the hope I have been given as a gift to others. I dreamt of stars and now I have found the sun of truth.

A Voice Is Like a Candle

There is no better way to understand our work than through knowledge of the will, resilience and determination to overcome anguish and pain that often characterize our clients. To read this book and listen to these voices is to gain that knowledge. Like candles the words flicker, sometimes brightly and urgently, and at other times burn dimly but steadily. They bring their messages from the darkest hours towards the light of day.

We exist to enable survivors of torture and organized violence to engage in a healing process to assert their own human dignity and worth. We advocate respect for human rights and are concerned for the health and well-being of survivors of torture and their families. We provide them with medical and social care, practical assistance and psychological and physical therapy.

We also document evidence of torture, provide training for health professionals and educate the public and decisionmakers. The Medical Foundation is a registered charity and the only one of its kind in the UK. We are dependent for our income on voluntary donations.

The Medical Foundation is a place where survivors of torture can feel that their experiences are believed and where they can safely express their grief and anger. We help victims of torture to find and recognize what helped them to survive, in particular their own inner resources. We try to help them build on those strengths and resources and to use them in facing the new difficulties and challenges of life in exile.

Their voice is the one thing suppressed and taken away in their own country. Even when times change and a new society is built, the voices of the past are often not given a place. In their country of exile people are, all too often, invisible or seen only as a burden. In this book they speak out and express their humanity.

I hope you will do more than read this book. We each have a voice, and that voice can be used for good or evil. Or it can simply be silent.

I hope, above all, that yours will not be silent. I hope that you will use your voice emphatically for good. It is the crescendo of all our small voices that may – even in your lifetime – put an end to tyranny.

Helen Bamber, OBE
Director, the Medical Foundation for the Care of Victims of
Torture

Sources

Babek
Permission granted by author

Loss

'XX' Manuel José Arce
This poem was originally published in *Index on Censorship* 1989, Vol. 18, no. 4. For information contact:
Tel: + 44 (171) 278 2313
Fax: + 44 (171) 278 1878
Email: contact@indexoncensorship.org
Or visit Index on the Web at http://www.oneworld.org/index-oc

'Quite Unfair and Cruel to Boot' Anon
This poem was originally published in *Index on Censorship* 1994, Vol. 23, no. 3. For information contact:
Tel: +44 (171) 278 2313
Fax: + 44 (171) 278 1878
Email: contact@indexoncensorship.org
Or visit Index on the Web at http://www.oneworld.org/index-oc

Last Letter to Osip Nadezhda Mandelstam
Translated by Max Hayward
Nadezhda Mandelstam: 'Last Letter' from *Hope Abandoned*. First published in Great Britain by Harvill in 1974. © Atheneum Publishers. © in the English translation Atheneum Publishers, New York, and Harvill 1973, 1994. Reproduced by permission of The Harvill Press.

Extract from *'Quatrain'* Ayshe Yanar
Translated by Richard McKane
We have tried to contact the author for permission but have so far been unsuccessful.

'Dear Prison Warden Xing', March 16, 1982 from *The Courage to Stand Alone* Wei Jingsheng
Translated by Kristina M. Torgeson
Translation copyright © 1997 by Wei Jingsheng. Used by permission of Viking Penguin, a division of Penguin Putnam Inc.

'*Walk*' Alfredo Cordal
Translated by Alfredo Cordal and Seth Sethna
Permission granted by the author, previously unpublished.

'*If Death. . .*' Miguel Huezo Mixco
Translated by Claribel Alegría and Darwin J. Flakoll
First published in *On the Front Line: Guerrilla Poems of El Salvador*, edited
and translated by Claribel Alegría and Darwin J. Flakoll. Curbstone Press,
1989. Translation © Claribel Alegría and Darwin J. Flakoll.

Loss: Testimony Wanjiku
Permission granted.

IDENTITY

'*In Hiding*' Erich Fried
Translated by Stuart Hood
First published in Great Britain in 1978 by John Calder (Publishers) Ltd.
Used by permission. Copyright © Erich Fried Estate. Translation © Stuart
Hood. All poems were originally published in German book form by Klaus
Wagenbach.

'*Silent, but . . .*' Tsuboi Shigeji
From 'One Cannot Ask Loneliness' from *The Penguin Book of Japanese Verse*,
edited and translated by Geoffrey Bowman and Anthony Thwaite (Penguin
Books, 1964). Translation copyright © Geoffrey Bowman and Anthony
Thwaite, 1964. Reproduced by Permission of Penguin Books Ltd.

Extract from *An Evil Cradling* Brian Keenan
First published in the United Kingdom by Hutchinson in 1992. Permission
granted by the author.

'*Half Poem*' Maria Jastrzebska
Taken from *GEN*, Issue 12/13, Refugee Women in Britain. We have been
unable to trace this person and publication.

Extract from '*On the Death of Ken Saro-Wiwa*'
Ken Saro-Wiwa
Previously unpublished. © Ken Saro-Wiwa. Reprinted by permission of
Ken Wiwa and Westwood Creative Artists.

'*Father*' Ediba-Bakira Kapic
Previously unpublished, permission granted by the author.

Identity: Testimony Chantal
Permission granted.

Impact

'Hope' Ariel Dorfman
Translated by Edie Grossman
Published in *Missing*, Amnesty International British Section. Permission granted by the author.

'Thieves' Primo Levi
From *Collected Poems* by Primo Levi, translated by Ruth Feldman and Brian Swann. Translation copyright © 1988 by Ruth Feldmann and Brian Swann. Reprinted by permission of Faber and Faber, Inc., a division of Farrar, Straus & Giroux, Inc.

Letters from Algeria Mourad
Collected by Philippe Bernard and Nathaniel Herzberg
Published in *Le Monde*, Paris, 19 November 1997.

'The People of Orpheus' María Eugenia Bravo Calderara
Translated by Ruth Valentine and Erif Reson
Previously unpublished; permission granted by the author.

'Every Day I Make Ready' Eduardo Embry Morales
Translated by Penelope Turpin
Published in *London Magazine* Oct/Nov 1975. Permission granted by the author.

'The Years We Didn't See the Dawn' Tin Moe
This poem was originally published in *Index on Censorship* 1994, Vol. 23, no. 3. For information contact:
Tel: + 44 (171) 278 2313
Fax: + 44 (171) 278 1878
Email: contact@indexoncensorship.org
Or visit Index on the Web at http://www.oneworld.org/index-oc

'The Executions' Sharnush Parsipur
Translated by Abbas Milani
Translation copyright © Abbas Milani
Published in *This Prison Where I Live* by Cassell, London, 1996
© International PEN.

'The True Prison' Ken Saro-Wiwa
Copyright © Ken Saro–Wiwa. Reprinted by permission of Ken Wiwa and Westwood Creative Artists.
Published in *This Prison Where I Live* by Cassell, London, 1996
© International PEN.

Impact: Testimony Fatma
Permission granted.

BYSTANDERS

'What Happens' Erich Fried
Translated by Stuart Hood
First published in Great Britain in 1978 by John Calder (Publishers) Ltd.
Copyright © Erich Fried Estate. Translation © Stuart Hood. All poems were
originally published in German book form by Klaus Wagenbach.

'Horizon' Nina Cassian
Translated by Andrea Deletant and Brenda Walker
Published in *An Anthology of Contemporary Romanian Poetry*, translated by
Brenda Walker and Andrea Deletant, by Forest Books 1984. Translations
© Andrea Deletant and Brenda Walker.

'Fears from Mikuyu Cells for Our Loves' Jack Mapanje
First published in *The Chattering Wagtails of Mikuyu Prison* by Heinemann
International Literature and Textbooks, Oxford 1993. © Jack Mapanje 1993.

'Their Behaviour' Dennis Brutus
Published in *Letters to Martha and Other Poems from a South African Prison*
by Heinemann, Oxford, 1968. © Dennis Brutus 1968.

'The Bystanders' Sheila Cassidy
Original piece written for this book; permission granted by the author.

SURVIVAL

'The Early Days of Torture' Alex Polari
Translated by Alicia and Nick Caistor
This poem was originally published in *Index on Censorship* 1979, no. 4. For
information contact:
Tel: + 44 (171) 278 2313
Fax: + 44 (171) 278 1878
Email: contact@indexoncensorship.org
Or visit Index on the Web at http://www.oneworld.org/index-oc
Reproduced with the permission of Nick Caistor.

Extract from *The Railway Man* Eric Lomax
First published in Great Britain by Jonathan Cape Ltd 1995. Permission
granted by Random House, London.

'Private Soldier' María Eugenia Bravo Calderara
Translated by Dinah Livingstone
First published in *Prayer in the National Stadium* by María Eugenia Bravo
Calderara by Katabasis, London 1992. © María Eugenia Bravo Calderara,
translation © Dinah Livingstone.

'A Short Journey with the Moon on a Dark Night' Ala Mehrzad
Previously unpublished; permission given by the author.

'The Embrace' Oktay Rifat
Translated by Ruth Christie
First published in *Voices of Memory: Selected Poems of Oktay Rifat*,
Rockingham Press, 1993.

Extract from *Prisoner of Mao: Three Scenes from a Labour Camp* Bao Ruowang and Rudolph Chelminski
It has proved impossible to track down the copyright holders for this
extract. If copyright has been infringed the publishers invite the copyright
holders to contact them in the first instance.

Extract from *Rue du Retour* Abdellatif Laabi
Translated by Jacqueline Kaye.
First published in English by Readers International Inc. and Readers
International England, 1989. English translation © Readers International
Inc. 1989.
First published in French, *Le Chemin des ordiales* by Editions Denoël, Paris,
1982.

'Words Can Save Lives' Ala Mehrzad
Previously unpublished; permission granted by the author.

Survival: Testimony Rad Baan
Permission granted.

EXILE

'The Good Immigrant' Maria Jastrzebska
From *GEN* Issue 12/13: Refugee Women in Britain. We have been unable to
trace this person and publication.

'Terminal Two' Ediba-Bakira Kapic
Previously unpublished; permission granted by the author.

'Exile Is an Island of No Return' Alfredo Cordal
Previously unpublished; permission granted by the author.

'The Unfamiliar Customs House' Liu Hongbin
Published in *China Now*, edited by Angie Knox. Permission granted by the
author.

'Siberia in My Soul' and a personal fax Taslima Nasrin
'Siberia in My Soul' originally published in *Index on Censorship* 1996, Vol.
25, no. 2. For information contact:
Tel: + 44 (171) 278 2313
Fax: + 44 (171) 278 1878
Email: contact@indexoncensorship.org
Or visit Index on the Web at http://www.oneworld.org/index-oc.
Permission granted by author.

'Emigrant's Lament' Bertolt Brecht
Translated by Edith Roseveare
This edition, including introduction and notes, copyright © 1976, 1979 by
Methuen, London Ltd. From *Bertolt Brecht Poems 1913–1956*, edited by John
Willet and Ralph Manheim with the cooperation of Erich Fried.
Reproduced by permission of Methuen and Routledge, Inc. First published
in Great Britain by Eyre Methuen 1976 by arrangement with Suhrkamp
Verlag, Frankfurt am Main. Copyright in the original poem © Suhrkamp
Verlag, Frankfurt am Main, 1967. Published in German as 'Klage des
Emigranten', GW 624 (German Collected Works) Ged 5.63 (Gedichte)
© Suhrkamp Verlag, Frankfurt am Main 1967.

Exile: Testimony Adnan
Permission granted.